The New Python Programming for Beginners

2021 EDITION

CONTENTS

Introduction

Configuring your Environment for Python

    Installing Python

        Choosing Python 2 or Python 3

        Windows Installation Instructions

        Mac Installation Instructions

        Linux Installation Instructions

    Preparing Your Computer for Python

        Running Python Programs

        Creating and Editing Python Source Code

        Downloading the Source Code Examples

    Review

    Resources

Chapter 1 - Variables and Strings

    Variables

    Strings

    Using Quotes within Strings

    Indexing

    Built-in Functions

        The print() Function

        The len() Function

String Methods

    The lower() String Method

    The upper() String Method

String Concatenation

Repeating Strings

The str() Function

Formatting Strings

Getting User Input

Review

Exercises

    Animal, Vegetable, Mineral

    Copy Cat

    What Did the Cat Say?

Resources

Review

Chapter 2 - Numbers, Math, and Comments

Numeric Operations

Strings and Numbers

The int() Function

The float() Function

Comments

Review

Exercises

    Calculate the Cost of Cloud Hosting

    Calculate the Cost of Cloud Hosting, Continued

Chapter 3 - Booleans and Conditionals

Comparators

Boolean Operators

Conditionals

Review

Exercises

    Walk, Drive, or Fly

Resources

Chapter 4 - Functions

Review

Exercises

    Fill in the Blank Word Game

Resources

Chapter 5 - Lists

Adding Items to a List

Slices

String Slices

Finding an Item in a List

Exceptions

Looping through a List

Sorting a List

List Concatenation

Ranges

Review

Exercises

    To-Do List

Resources

Chapter 6 - Dictionaries

Adding Items to a Dictionary

Removing Items from a Dictionary

Finding a Key in a Dictionary

Finding a Value in a Dictionary

Looping through a Dictionary

Nesting Dictionaries

Review

Exercises

    Interesting Facts

Resources

Chapter 7 - Tuples

Switching between Tuples and Lists

Looping through a Tuple

Tuple Assignment

Review

Exercises

    Airport Codes

Resources

Chapter 8 - Reading from and Writing to Files

File Position

Closing a File

Automatically Closing a File

Reading a File One Line at a Time

File Modes

Writing to a File

Binary Files

Exceptions

Review

Exercises

    Line Numbers

    Alphabetize

Resources

Chapter 9 - Modules and the Python Standard Library

Modules

Peeking Inside a Module

The Module Search Path

The Python Standard Library

Creating Your Own Modules

Using main

Review

Exercises

    What Did the Cat Say, Redux

Resources

Conclusion

Appendix

Appendix A: Trademarks

Introduction

Knowing where to start when learning a new skill can be a challenge, especially when the topic seems so vast. There can be so much information available that you can't even decide where to start. Or worse, you start down the path of learning and quickly discover too many concepts, programming examples, and nuances that aren't explained. This kind of experience is frustrating and leaves you with more questions than answers.

Python Programming for Beginners doesn't make any assumptions about your background or knowledge of computer programming or the Python language. You need no prior knowledge to benefit from this book. You will be guided step by step using a logical and systematic approach. As new concepts, code, or jargon are encountered they are explained in plain language, making it easy for anyone to understand.

Throughout the book you will presented with many examples and various Python programs.

Let's get started.

Configuring your Environment for Python

Installing Python

Choosing Python 2 or Python 3

If you are starting a new project or are just learning Python I highly recommend using Python 3. Python 3.0 was released in 2008 and at this point the Python 2.x series is considered legacy. However, there are a lot of Python 2 programs that are still in use today and you may encounter them from time to time. The good news is that the Python 2.7 release bridges the gap between Python 2 and Python 3. Much of the code written for Python 3 will work on Python 2.7. However, that same code will most likely not run unmodified on Python versions 2.6 and lower.

Long story short, if at all possible use the latest version of Python available. If you must use Python 2, use Python 2.7 as it is compatible with all Python 2 code and much of Python 3. The primary reason to choose Python 2 over Python 3 is if your project requires third-party software that is not yet compatible with Python 3.

Windows Installation Instructions

By default, Python does not come installed on the Windows operating system. Download the Python installer from the Python downloads page at https://www.python.org/downloads. Click on "Download Python 3.x.x." to download the installer. Double click the file to start the installation process. Simply keep clicking on "Next" to accept all of the defaults. If you are asked if you want to install software on this computer, click on "Yes." To exit the installer and complete the Python installation, click on "Finish."

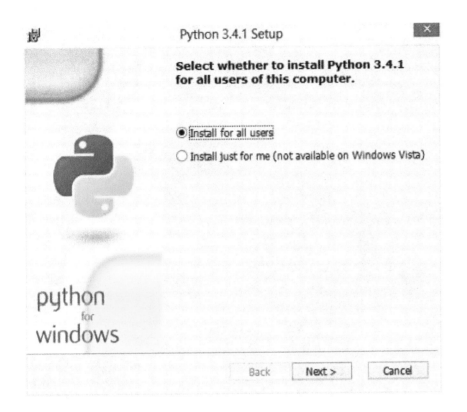

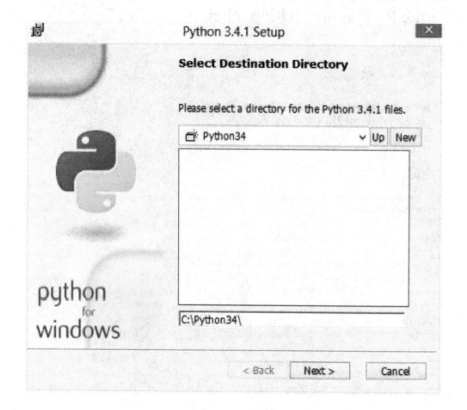

Python 3.4.1 Setup

Install Python 3.4.1

Please wait while the Installer installs Python 3.4.1. This may take several
minutes.

Status: Copying new files

< Back   Next >   Cancel

Mac Installation Instructions

At the time of this writing the Mac operating system ships with Python 2. In order to use the latest version of Python, you will need to download and install it. Visit the Python downloads page at https://www.python.org/downloads and click on "Download Python 3.x.x." Double click on the file you just downloaded to access the contents of the disk image. Run the installer by double clicking on the "Python.mpkg" file. If you encounter a message stating that "Python.mpkg can't be opened because it is from an unidentified developer," you will need to control-click the Python.mpkg file. Next, select "Open with ..." and finally click on "Installer." When you are asked if you are sure you want to open it, click "Open." If you are asked to enter an administrator's username and password, please do so.

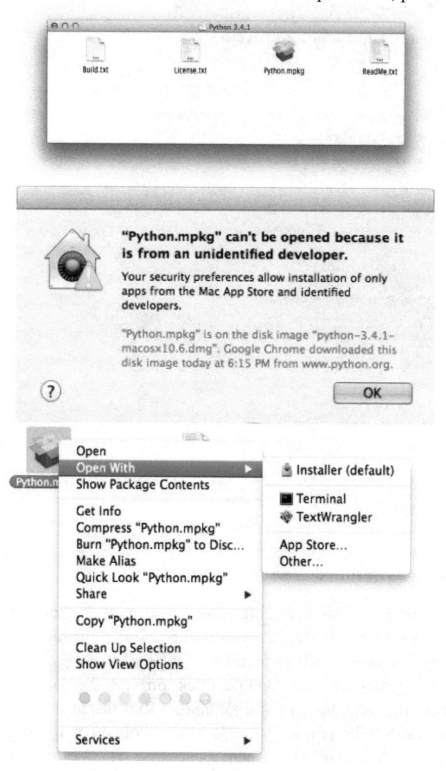

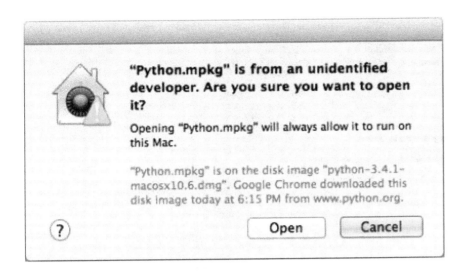

Click through the installer and accept all of the defaults.

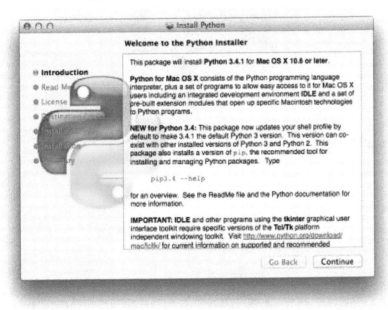

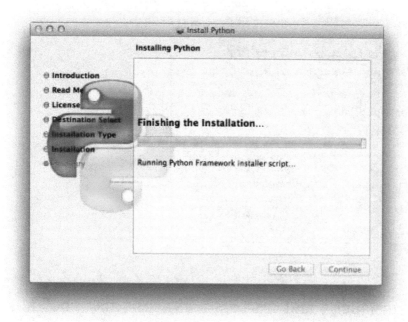

You will now have a Python folder that resides in the Applications folder. In the Python folder you will find a link to IDLE, the Integrated DeveLopment Environment, and a link to some Python documentation. In addition to accessing Python from IDLE, you can open up the Terminal application, located at /Application/Utilities/Terminal, and run python3 . Later in this chapter you will learn how to run Python programs using IDLE and the command line.

```
[jason@mac ~]$ which python3
/Library/Frameworks/Python.framework/Versions/3.4/bin/python3
[jason@mac ~]$ python3 --version
Python 3.4.1
```

Linux Installation Instructions

Some Linux distributions ship with just Python 2 installed. However, it is becoming more and more common to see Python 2 and Python 3 installed by default. To determine if you have Python installed, open a terminal emulator application and type python --version and python3 --version at the command prompt. In many cases the python command will actually be Python 2 and there will be a python3 command for running Python 3.

```
[jason@linuxbox ~]$ python --version
Python 2.7.6
[jason@linuxbox ~]$ python3 --version
Python 3.4.1
```

If python or python3 is not installed on your Linux system you will see a "command not found" error message. In the following example, Python 2 is installed but Python3 is not.

```
[jason@linuxbox ~]$ python --version
Python 2.7.6
[jason@linuxbox ~]$ python3 --version
python3: command not found
```

Installing Python on Debian Based Linux Distributions

To install Python 3 on Debian based distributions such Debian, Ubuntu, and Linux Mint, run apt-get install -y python3 idle3 . Installing software requires root privileges so execute the apt command as the root user or precede the command with sudo . Note that sudo will only work if it has been configured, either by the distribution, you, or the system administrator. Here is an example of installing Python 3 on an Ubuntu Linux system using sudo.

```
[jason@ubuntu ~]$ sudo apt-get install -y python3 idle3
...
Setting up python3
[jason@ubuntu ~]$ python3 --version
3.4.1
```

To perform the installation as root, log into the Linux system as root or switch to the root user using the su - command.

```
[jason@ubuntu ~]$ su -
Password:
[root@ubuntu ~]# apt-get install -y python3 idle3
...
Setting up python3
[root@ubuntu ~]# python3 --version
3.4.1
[root@ubuntu ~]# exit
[jason@ubuntu ~]$
```

Installing Python on RPM Based Linux Distributions

For RPM based Linux distributions such as CentOS, Fedora, RedHat, and Scientific Linux attempt to install Python 3 using the yum install -y python3 python3-tools command. Be sure to run the command as root or precede it with sudo as installing software requires root privileges. Note that sudo will only work if it has been configured, either by the distribution, you, or the system administrator. Here is an example of installing Python 3 on a Fedora Linux system using sudo.

```
[jason@fedora ~]$ sudo yum install -y python3 python3-tools
...
Complete!
[jason@fedora ~]$ python3 --version
3.4.1
```

If you get an error message like "No package python3 available" or "Error: Nothing to do," then you will have to install Python3 from source code. Start out by installing the tools required to build and install Python by running yum groupinstall -y 'development tools' with root privileges. Next, install the remaining dependencies by running yum install -y zlib-dev openssl-devel sqlite-devel bzip2-devel tk-devel .

```
[jason@centos ~]$ sudo yum groupinstall -y 'development tools'
...
Complete!
[jason@centos ~]$ sudo yum install -y zlib-dev openssl-devel sqlite-devel bzip2-devel tk-devel
...
Complete!
```

Next, visit the Python downloads page at https://www.python.org/downloads and click on "Download Python 3.x.x." In a terminal emulator application navigate to the directory where Python was just saved. Extract the contents of the file using tar xf Python*z . Change into the directory that was created from performing the extraction with cd Python-* . Run ./configure followed by make and finally, as root, run make install . If sudo is configured on your system you can run sudo make install . This process will install Python 3 into the /usr/local/bin directory.

```
[jason@centos ~]$ cd ~/Downloads
[jason@centos ~/Downloads]$ tar xf Python*z
[jason@centos ~/Downloads/Python-3.4.1]$ cd Python-*
[jason@centos ~/Downloads/Python-3.4.1]$ ./configure
...
creating Makefile
[jason@centos ~/Downloads/Python-3.4.1]$ make
...
[jason@centos ~/Downloads/Python-3.4.1]$ sudo make install
...
[jason@centos ~/Downloads/Python-3.4.1]$ which python3
/usr/local/bin/python3
[jason@centos ~/Downloads/Python-3.4.1]$ python3 --version
Python 3.4.1
```

If you are interested in learning more about the Linux operating system I encourage you to read *Linux for Beginners* . You can get a copy by visiting http://www.LinuxTrainingAcademy.com/linux or http://www.amazon.com/gp/product/B00HNC1AXY.

Preparing Your Computer for Python

It's important for you to run the Python interpreter interactively as well as execute existing Python programs. When using the Python interpreter interactively you can type in Python commands and receive immediate feedback. It's an excellent way to experiment with Python and answer any of your "I wonder what happens if I were to do this" type of questions. By the way, Python is called an interpreter because it translates the Python language into a format that is understood by the underlying operating system and hardware.

There are two ways to start the Python interpreter. The first way is to the launch the IDLE application. IDLE stands for "Integrated DeveLopment Environment." The other way to start the Python interpreter is from the command line. In Windows start the Command Prompt and type `python`. In Mac and Linux execute `python3` from the command line. To exit the Python interpreter type `exit()` or `quit()`. You can also exit the interpreter by typing `Ctrl-d` on Mac and Linux and `Ctrl-z` on Windows. Here is an example of running the Python interpreter from the command line on a Mac system.

```
[jason@mac ~]$ python3
Python 3.4.1 (v3.4.1:c0e311e010fc, May 18 2014, 00:54:21)
[GCC 4.2.1 (Apple Inc. build 5666) (dot 3)] on darwin
Type "help", "copyright", "credits" or "license" for more information.
>>> print('Hello')
Hello
>>> exit()
[jason@mac ~]$
```

Don't worry about the `print('Hello')` line just yet. You will learn the details of that and other commands in the following chapters. For now, just know that you can execute the Python command or start the IDLE application to interact directly with the Python interpreter.

Running Python Programs

In addition to using the Python interpreter interactively, you will need a way to create, save, and execute Python programs. Python programs are simply text files that contain a series of Python commands. By convention Python programs end in a .py extension.

Running Python Programs on Windows

One way to run a Python program on Windows is navigate to the location of the file using the File Explorer and double click it. The disadvantage of using this method is that when the program exits the program's window is closed. You may not be able to see the output generated by the program, especially if no user interaction is required. A better way to run Python programs is by using the command line, sometimes called the Command Prompt in Windows.

First, let's make sure the Python interpreter is in our path. Using the File Explorer, navigate to the folder where you installed Python. If you accepted the defaults during the installation the path will be C:\PythonNN , where NN is the version number. For example, if you installed Python 3.4 it would be C:\Python34 . Next, navigate to the Tools folder and finally to the Scripts folder. Double click on the win_add2path file. The full path to this file is C:\Python34\Tools\Scripts\win_add2path.py . You will see a window pop up briefly and then disappear.

Locate the Command Prompt application and open it. There are various ways to do this depending on what version of Windows you are using. This following procedure will work on most, if not all, versions of windows. Press and hold the Windows key and type r . A prompt will open. Now type cmd and press enter.

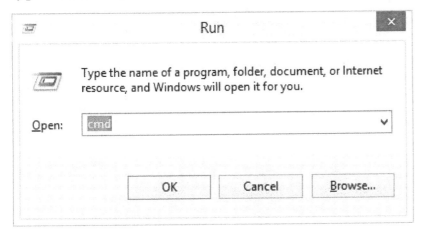

You can also search for the Command Prompt. For Windows Vista and Windows 7 click the Start button, type "cmd" in the search box, and press Enter. For Windows 8, click on the search icon, type "cmd" in the search box, and press Enter.

Once you have opened the Command Prompt, you can run Python interactively by typing python or run a Python application by typing python program_name.py . If you get an error message like "python' is not recognized as an internal or external command, operable program or batch file," reboot your computer and try again.

The following example demonstrates running Python interactively from the command line and then running the hello.py program.

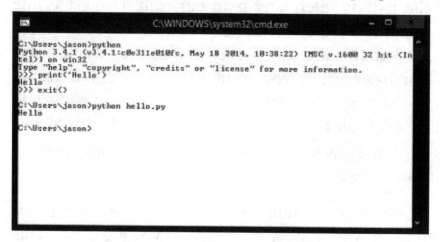

Running Python Programs on Mac and Linux

In Mac and Linux you can execute a Python program by running python3 program_name.py from the command line. The Python interpreter will load and execute the code in the file that follows the Python command.

Here are the contents of the hello.py file.

```
print('Hello')
```

Here is what you will see when you run the program.

```
[jason@mac ~]$ python3 hello.py
Hello
[jason@mac ~]$
```

In addition to supplying a Python file to the python 3 command, you can execute the file directly by setting the execute bit on the file and specifying Python in the interpreter directive on the first line. To set the execute bit on the file run chmod +x program_name.py from the command line. To set the interpreter directive make sure #!/usr/bin/env python3 is the first line in the Python file. Now you can run the Python program by using a relative or an absolute path to the file.

Here are the contents of the hello2.py file.

```
#!/usr/bin/env python3
print('Hello')
```

The following example demonstrates how to set the executable bit on hello2.py , execute it using a relative path, execute it using an absolute path, and execute it by supplying it as an argument to the python 3 command.

```
[jason@mac ~]$ chmod +x hello2.py
[jason@mac ~]$ ./hello2.py
Hello
[jason@mac ~]$ /Users/jason/hello2.py
Hello
[jason@mac ~]$ python3 hello2.py
Hello
[jason@mac ~]$
```

Note that is safe to include the interpreter directive even if the program will be executed on a Windows system. Windows will simply ignore that line and execute the remaining Python code.

Creating and Editing Python Source Code

The IDLE application not only allows you to run the Python interpreter interactively, it allows you to create, edit, and execute Python programs. To create a new Python program, go to the "File" menu and select "New File." To open an existing Python file, go the "File" menu and select "Open." You can now type in or edit your Python program. Save your program by accessing the "File" menu and selecting "Save." To run the program press "F5" or go to the "Run" menu and select "Run Module."

```
Python 3.4.1 Shell                          Python 3.4.1: Hello.py...
Python 3.4.1 (v3.4.1:c0e311e010fc, May 18 2014,  00:54:21)    print('Hello')
[GCC 4.2.1 (Apple Inc. build 5666) (dot 3)] on darwin
Type "copyright", "credits" or "license()" for more information.
>>> ============================ RESTART ===========================
================================
>>>
Hello
>>>
                                   Ln: 7 Col: 4               Ln: 2 Col: 0
```

Since Python source code is nothing more than a text file you are not limited to the IDLE editor. You can use your favorite text editor to create Python files and execute them from the command line as previously discussed. There are many great text editors available. Here are some of my favorite editors for Windows, Mac, and Linux.

Windows

- Geany: http://www.geany.org/

- JEdit: http://www.jedit.org/

- Komodo Edit: http://komodoide.com/komodo-edit/

- Notepad++: http://notepad-plus-plus.org/

Mac

- JEdit: http://www.jedit.org/

- Komodo Edit: http://komodoide.com/komodo-edit/

- Sublime Text: http://www.sublimetext.com/

- TextWrangler: http://www.barebones.com/products/textwrangler/

Linux

- Emacs: https://www.gnu.org/software/emacs/

- Geany: http://www.geany.org/

- JEdit: http://www.jedit.org/

- Komodo Edit: http://komodoide.com/komodo-edit/

- Sublime Text: http://www.sublimetext.com/

- Vim: http://www.vim.org/

Note: When writing Python source code you will be using an indentation of four spaces. I recommend configuring your editor to insert four spaces when you press the tab key. Also, configure your editor to save files using Unix line endings. This ensure your programs are cross-platform compatible. You will then be able to use the same file on Windows, Mac, and Linux.

Downloading the Source Code Examples

Even though it may be easier to simply look at and run the code examples, it is more beneficial for you to take the extra time to type them out yourself. By typing the source code in it reinforces what you are learning. It also gives you the practical experience of fixing issues that arise when you are creating code of your own. For example, you will have to find and spot spelling mistakes and find the syntax errors in your code. Details like spacing, spelling, capitalization, and punctuation marks are crucial to writing functional programs. Of course, if you get stuck on an exercise look at the examples and try to spot the differences between your code and the code you have downloaded and read in this book.

Review

- Install Python. Use Python 3 unless you have a need to use Python 2. If you do, use Python 2.7.

- Run Python interactively by using IDLE or by executing the Python command at the command line. Use python for Windows and python3 for Mac and Linux.

- Run Python programs in IDLE by pressing "F5" or by navigating to the "Run" menu and selecting "Run Module." You can also run Python programs from the command line by executing the Python command followed by a Python file. For Windows the format is python program_name.py. For Mac and Linux the format is python3 program_name.py.

- Use IDLE to edit your Python source code or use a text editor of your choice.

Resources

- Integrated Development Environments for Python: https://wiki.python.org/moin/IntegratedDevelopmentEnvironments

- Open the Command Prompt in Windows: http://www.wikihow.com/Open-the-Command-Prompt-in-Windows

- Python 3 Installation Video for Linux: https://www.youtube.com/watch?v=RLPYBxfAud4

- Python 3 Installation Video for Mac: https://www.youtube.com/watch?v=EZ_6tmtbDSM

- Python 3 Installation Video for Windows: https://www.youtube.com/watch?v=CihHoWzmFe4

- Should I use Python 2 or Python 3 for my development activity? https://wiki.python.org/moin/Python2orPython3

- Source Code Examples for this Book: http://www.LinuxTrainingAcademy.com/python-for-beginners

Chapter 1 - Variables and Strings

Variables

Variables are storage locations that have a name. Said another way, variables are name-value pairs. You can assign values to a variable and recall those values by the variable name. To assign a value to a variable, use the equals sign. The format is `variable_name = value` .

In this example the value of `apple` is assigned to the variable called `fruit` .

```
fruit = 'apple'
```

You can change the value of a variable by reassigning it. Here is how to set the value of the `fruit` variable to the value of `orange` .

```
fruit = 'orange'
```

Note that there is nothing significant about the variable named `fruit` . We could have easily used `produce` , `crop` , `food` , or almost any other variable name that you can think of. When choosing a variable name, pick something that represents the data the variable will hold. You may know what a variable named `x` represents today, but if you come back to the code a few months from now you may not. However, if you encounter a variable named `fruit` chances are you can guess what data it will hold.

Variable names are case sensitive. The variables `Fruit` and `fruit` are two distinct variables. By convention, variables are in all lower case letters, but it is not a requirement. Variable names must start with a letter. They can contain numbers, but variable names cannot start with a number. You can also use the underscore (_) character in variable names. You cannot use a hyphen (-), plus sign (+) and other various symbols in variable names. Whenever you get the urge to use a hyphen, use an underscore instead.

Here are some examples of valid variable names.

```
first3letters = 'ABC'
first_three_letters = 'ABC'
firstThreeLetters = 'ABC'
```

Strings

A string is used to represent text. In the previous examples the text `apple`, `orange`, and `ABC` are strings. In Python strings are surrounded by quotes. Let's revisit our first example of creating a variable named `fruit` and assigning it the string `apple`.

```
fruit = 'apple'
```

Strings can also be encapsulated in double quotes.

```
fruit = "apple"
```

Using Quotes within Strings

Python expects matching quotation marks for strings. When you start a string definition with a double quotation mark, the next double quotation mark that Python encounters is interpreted as the end of the string. The same is true for single quotation marks. If you start a string with a single quotation mark, the next single quotation mark represents the end of that string.

If you want to include double quotes in a string you can place them inside single quotes as in the following example.

```
sentence = 'She said, "That is a great tasting apple!"'
```

If you want to include single quotes in a string, enclose the string in double quotation marks.

```
sentence = "That's a great tasting apple!"
```

What if you wanted to use both single and double quotes in the same string? At this point you need to escape the offending quotation character by prepending a backslash (\ ). The next example demonstrates how to escape the following string when using double and single quotes.

She said, "That's a great tasting apple!"

```
sentence_in_double = "She said, \"That's a great tasting apple!\""
sentence_in_single = 'She said, "That\'s a great tasting apple!"'
```

Indexing

Each character in a string is assigned an index. String indices are zero based, meaning that the first character in a string has an index of 0, the second character has an index of 1, etc.

```
String: a p p l e
Index: 0 1 2 3 4
```

To access the character at a given index append [N] to a string where N is the index number. The following example creates a variable named a and assigns it the character in position 0 of the string apple . Likewise, a variable of e is created using the character from position 4 of apple .

```
a = 'apple'[0]
e = 'apple'[4]
```

Since variables are simply names that represent their values, the [N] syntax will also work with variables. In the following example   first_char will be assigned the value a .

```
fruit = 'apple'
first_char = fruit[0]
```

Built-in Functions

A function is a section of reusable code that performs an action. A function has a name and is called, or executed, by that name. Optionally, functions can accept arguments and return data.

The print() Function

Python includes many built-in functions, one of which is the print() function. When a value is provided as an argument to the print() function it displays that value to the screen. You can supply values directly to the print statement or pass in variables.

```
fruit = 'apple'
print(fruit)
print('orange')
```

Output:

```
apple
orange
```

The len() Function

Another built-in function is the len() function. When a string is provided as an argument to the len() function it returns the length of that string. Said another way, len() returns the number of characters in a string.

In this example the value of apple is assigned to the variable named fruit. Next we assign the result of len(fruit) to the fruit_len variable. Finally we display that value to the screen using the print(fruit_len) function.

```
fruit = 'apple'
fruit_len = len(fruit)
print(fruit_len)
```

Output:

```
5
```

You can also pass the len() function to the print() function and skip the intermediary step of assigning it to a variable. This works because len(fruit) is evaluated first and its value is used by the print() function.

```
fruit = 'apple'
print(len(fruit))
```

Output:

```
5
```

You can even skip using variables all together.

```
print(len('apple'))
```

Output:

```
5
```

String Methods

Without going too in depth on the subject of Object Oriented Programming (OOP), it is helpful to understand a couple of concepts before proceeding. The first thing to know is that everything in Python is an object. Also, every object has a type. You have already been learning about the string data type and we will cover other types throughout the course of this book.

Let's get back to strings. For example, 'apple' is an object with a type of "str," which is short for string. Said another way, 'apple' is a string object. If we assign the value of apple to the variable fruit using fruit = 'apple' , then fruit is also a string object. Remember that variables are names that represent their values.

As previously mentioned, a function is a section of reusable code that performs an action. Thus far you have been using built-in functions like print() and len() . Objects also have functions, but they are not called functions. They are called methods. Methods are functions that are run against an object. To call a method on an object, follow the object with a period, then the method name, and finally a set of parenthesis. Enclose any parameters in the parenthesis.

The lower() String Method

The lower() method of a string object returns a copy of the string in all lower case letters.

```
fruit = 'Apple'
print(fruit.lower())
```

Output:

```
apple
```

The upper() String Method

The upper() string method returns a copy of the string in all upper case letters.

```
fruit = 'Apple'
print(fruit.upper())
```

Output:

```
APPLE
```

String Concatenation

To concatenate, or combine, two strings use the plus sign. You can think of this as adding strings together. You can concatenate multiple strings by using additional plus signs and strings. In the following example notice how spaces are included in the strings. String concatenation only combines the strings as they are.

```
print('I ' + 'love ' + 'Python.')
print('I' + ' love' + ' Python.')
```

Output:

```
I love Python.
I love Python.
```

If you do not include extra spaces, it would look like this.

```
print('I' + 'love' + 'Python.')
```

Output:

```
IlovePython.
```

The following example demonstrates string concatenation using variables.

```
first = 'I'
second = 'love'
third = 'Python'
sentence = first + ' ' + second + ' ' + third + '.'
print(sentence)
```

Output:

```
I love Python.
```

Repeating Strings

When working with strings, the asterisk is the repetition operator. The format is `'string' * number_of_times_to_repeat`. For example, if you want to display a hyphen ten times, use `'-' * 10`.

```
print('-' * 10)
```

Output:

```
----------
```

You don't have to use repetition with just single character strings.

```
happiness = 'happy ' * 3
print(happiness)
```

Output:

```
happy happy happy
```

The str() Function

In an upcoming chapter you will be learning about number data types. For now, just know that unlike strings, numbers are not enclosed in quotation marks. To concatenate a string with a number, first convert the number to a string with the built-in str() function. The str() function turns non-strings, such as numbers, into strings.

```
version = 3
print('I love Python ' + str(version) + '.')
```

Output:

```
I love Python 3.
```

Here is what happens when a number is not converted to a string before concatenation is attempted.

```
version = 3
print('I love Python ' + version + '.')
```

Output:

```
  File "string_example.py", line 2, in <module>
    print('I love Python ' + version)
TypeError: Can't convert 'int' object to str implicitly
```

Formatting Strings

Instead of concatenating strings to produce the format you desire, you can call the format() method on a string. Create placeholders, also known as format fields, by using curly braces in the string and pass in values for those fields to format() .

By default the first pair of curly braces will be replaced by the first value passed to format() , the second pair of curly braces will be replaced by the second value passed to format() , and so on. Here is an example.

```
print('I {} Python.'.format('love'))
print('{} {} {}'.format('I', 'love', 'Python.'))
```

Output:

```
I love Python.
I love Python.
```

Notice that when you pass multiple objects to a function or method you separate them using a comma. format('I', 'love', 'Python.') .

You can explicitly specify which positional parameter will be used for a format field by providing a number inside the braces. {0} will be replaced with the first item passed to format() , {1} will be replaced by the second item passed in, etc.

```
print('I {0} {1}. {1} {0}s me.'.format('love', 'Python'))
```

Output:

```
I love Python. Python loves me.
```

Here is a formatting example that uses variables.

```
first = 'I'
second = 'love'
third = 'Python'
print('{} {} {}.'.format(first, second, third))
```

Output:

```
I love Python.
```

We can now rewrite our previous example that combined strings and numbers using the format() method. This eliminates the need to use the str() function.

```
version = 3
print('I love Python {}.'.format(version))
```

Output:

```
I love Python 3.
```

You can also supply a format specification. Format specifications are contained within the curly braces and begin with a colon. To create a field with a minimum character width supply a number following the colon. The format field of {0:8} translates to "use the first value provided to format() and make it at least eight characters wide." The format field of {1:8} means "use the second value provided to format() and make it at least eight characters wide." This method can be used to create tables, for instance.

```
print('{0:8} | {1:8}'.format('Fruit', 'Quantity'))
print('{0:8} | {1:8}'.format('Apple', 3))
print('{0:8} | {1:8}'.format('Oranges', 10))
```

Output:

```
Fruit    | Quantity
Apple    |        3
Oranges  |       10
```

To control the alignment use < for left, ^ for center, and > for right. If no alignment is specified, left alignment is assumed. Building on our previous example, let's left align the numbers.

```
print('{0:8} | {1:<8}'.format('Fruit', 'Quantity'))
print('{0:8} | {1:<8}'.format('Apple', 3))
print('{0:8} | {1:<8}'.format('Oranges', 10))
```

Output:

```
Fruit   | Quantity
Apple   | 3
Oranges | 10
```

You can also specify a data type. The most common case is to use `f` which represents a float. Floats, or floating point numbers, will be covered in detail in the next chapter. You can specify the number of decimal places by using `.Nf` where `N` is the number of decimal places. A common currency format would be `.2f` which specifies two decimal places. Here is what our table might look like after we take a couple of bites out of an apple.

```
print('{0:8} | {1:<8}'.format('Fruit', 'Quantity'))
print('{0:8} | {1:<8.2f}'.format('Apple', 2.33333))
print('{0:8} | {1:<8.2f}'.format('Oranges', 10))
```

Output:

```
Fruit   | Quantity
Apple   | 2.33
Oranges | 10.00
```

Getting User Input

Use the built-in function input() to accept standard input. By default, standard input comes from a person typing at a keyboard. This allows you to prompt the user for input. In advanced cases standard input can come from other sources. For example, you can send the output from one command as the standard input to another command using pipes. (For more info on this topic refer to *Linux for Beginners* at http://www.linuxtrainingacademy.com/linux.)

You can pass in a prompt to display to the input() function.

```
fruit = input('Enter a name of a fruit: ')
print('{} is a lovely fruit.'.format(fruit))
```

Output:

```
Name a fruit: apple
apple is a lovely fruit.
```

Review

- Variables are names that store values.

- Variables must start with a letter, but may contain numbers and underscores.

- Assign values to variables using the variable_name = value syntax.

- Strings are surrounded by quotation marks.

- Each character in a string is assigned an index.

- A function is reusable code that performs an action.

  - Built-in functions:

  - print( ) : Displays values.

  - len( ) : Returns the length of an item.

  - str( ) : Returns a string object.

  - input( ) : Reads a string.

- Everything in Python is an object.

- Objects can have methods.

- Methods are functions that operate on an object.

  - String methods:

  - uppper( ) : Returns a copy of the string in uppercase.

  - lower( ) : Returns a copy of the string in lowercase.

  - format( ) : Returns a formatted version of the string.

Exercises

Animal, Vegetable, Mineral

Write a Python program that uses three variables. The variables in your program will be animal, vegetable, and mineral. Assign a string value to each one of the variables. Your program should display "Here is an animal, a vegetable, and a mineral." Next, display the value for animal, followed by vegetable, and finally mineral. Each one of the values should be printed on their own line. Your program will display four lines in total.

Sample Output:

```
Here is an animal, a vegetable, and a mineral.
cat
broccoli
gold
```

I encourage you to create a Python program the produces the above output before continuing. For the remainder of this book the solutions to the exercises will follow the exercise description and sample output. If you want to attempt the exercise on your own -- and I encourage you to do so -- stop reading now.

Solution

```
animal = 'cat'
vegetable = 'broccoli'
mineral = 'gold'

print('Here is an animal, a vegetable, and a mineral.')
print(animal)
print(vegetable)
print(mineral)
```

Copy Cat

Write a Python program that prompts the user for input and simply repeats what the user entered.

Sample output:

```
Please type something and press enter: Hello there!
You entered:
Hello there!
```

Here is one possible solution. Your program should look fairly similar, but you may have used a different variable name, for example. If you reproduced the previous output, you're doing great!

```
user_input = input('Please type something and press enter: ')
print('You entered:')
print(user_input)
```

What Did the Cat Say?

Write a Python program that prompts for input and displays a cat "saying" what was provided by the user. Place the input provided by the user inside a speech bubble. Make the speech bubble expand or contract to fit around the input provided by the user.

Sample output:

```
             _____
          < Pet me and I will purr. >
             ---------------
            /
   /\_/\ /
  ( o.o )
   > ^ <
```

Solution

```
text = input('What would you like the cat to say? ')
text_length = len(text)

print('          {}'.format('_' * text_length))
print('       < {} >'.format(text))
print('          {}'.format('-' * text_length))
print('        /')
print(' /\_/\ /')
print('( o.o )')
print(' > ^ <')
```

Output:

```
What would you like the cat to say? Meow

          _____
        < Meow >
          ---
        /
 /\_/\ /
 ( o.o )
 > ^ <
```

Resources

- Common String Operations: https://docs.python.org/3/library/string.html

- input( ) documentation: https://docs.python.org/3/library/functions.html?highlight=input#input

- len( ) documentation: https://docs.python.org/3/library/functions.html?highlight=input#len

- print( ) documentation: https://docs.python.org/3/library/functions.html?highlight=input#print

- str( ) documentation: https://docs.python.org/3/library/functions.html?highlight=input#func-str

Chapter 2 - Numbers, Math, and Comments

If you would like to see a video I created for you that covers the concepts in this chapter and includes a live programming demonstration visit:

http://www.LinuxTrainingAcademy.com/python-math

In the previous chapter you learned how to create strings by enclosing text in quotation marks. Numbers in Python require no such special treatment. When you want to use a number, simply include it in your source code. If you want to assign a number to a variable use the format of variable_name = number as in this example.

```
integer = 42
float = 4.2
```

Python supports integers as well as floating point numbers. Integers are whole numbers, or numbers without a decimal point. Floating point numbers always contain a decimal point. The data type for integers is int , while the data type for floating point numbers is float .

Numeric Operations

The Python interpreter can perform several operations with numbers. The following table lists the most commonly used numeric operations.

Symbol	Operation
+	add
-	subtract
*	multiply
/	divide
**	exponentiate
%	modulo

You're probably familiar with + , - , * , and / . The ** operator is for exponentiation, which means to "raise to the power of." For example, 2 ** 4 means "2 raised to the power of 4." This is equivalent to 2 * 2 * 2 * 2 and results in an outcome of 16 .

The percent sign performs the modulo operation. It simply returns the remainder. For example, 3 % 2 is 1 because three divided by two is one with a remainder of one. 4 % 2 returns 0 since four divided by two is two with a remainder of zero.

Python allows you to   perform mathematical calculations right in the interpreter.

```
[jason@mac ~]$ python3
Python 3.4.1 (v3.4.1:c0e311e010fc, May 18 2014, 00:54:21)
[GCC 4.2.1 (Apple Inc. build 5666) (dot 3)] on darwin
Type "help", "copyright", "credits" or "license" for more information.
>>> 1 + 2
3
>>> exit()
[jason@mac ~]$
```

You can also assign the resulting value of a mathematical operation to a variable as in this example.

```
sum = 1 + 2
difference = 100 - 1
product = 3 * 4
quotient = 8 / 2
power = 2 ** 4
remainder = 3 % 2

print('Sum: {}'.format(sum))
print('Difference: {}'.format(difference))
print('Product: {}'.format(product))
print('Quotient: {}'.format(quotient))
print('Power: {}'.format(power))
print('Remainder:  {}'.format(remainder))
```

Output:

```
Sum: 3
Difference: 99
Product: 12
Quotient: 4.0
Power: 16
Remainder: 1
```

Even though the result of 8 / 2 is the integer 4 , you will notice that the floating point number 4.0 was in the output created by the previous example. The division operator (/) performs floating point division and will always return a floating point number. Also be aware that if you add an integer to a floating point number the result will be a float.

The following example demonstrations how you can even perform mathematical operations using variables.

```
sum = 1 + 2
difference = 100 - 1
new_number = sum + difference
print(new_number)
print(sum / sum)
print(sum + 1)
```

Output:

102
1.0
4

Strings and Numbers

This example creates a variable named quantity and assigns it the numeric value of 3 . It also creates a variable named quantity_string and assigns it the string 3 .

```
quantity = 3
quantity_string = '3'
```

If you try to perform a mathematical operation against a string you will encounter an error. Just be aware that if you surround a number in quotes it becomes a string.

```
quantity_string = '3'
total = quantity_string + 2
```

Output:

```
Traceback (most recent call last):
  File "string_test.py", line 2, in <module>
    total = quantity_string + 2
TypeError: Can't convert 'int' object to str implicitly
```

The int() Function

To convert a string into an integer use the int() function and pass in the string to convert.

```
quantity_string = '3'
total = int(quantity_string) + 2
print(total)
```

Output:

```
5
```

The float() Function

To convert a string into a floating point number use the float() function and pass in the string to convert.

```
quantity_string = '3'
quantity_float = float(quantity_string)
print(quantity_float)
```

Output:

```
3.0
```

Comments

Comments are for the benefit of us humans. Python will ignore any comments it encounters. Comments give you a way to document your code. It can help summarize what is about to happen in a complex piece of code, for example. If you or a fellow programmer need to look at the code at a later date it can help quickly explain what the intention of the code was when it was written.

A single line comment is prefixed with an octothorpe (#), also known as a pound sign, number sign, or hash.

```
# This is a comment. Python ignores comments.
```

You can chain multiple single line comments together.

```
# The following code:
#    Computes the hosting costs for one server.
#    Determines the duration of hosting that can be purchased given a budget.
```

You can also create multi-line comments using triple quotes. The comment begins right after the first set of triple quotes and ends right before the next set of triple quotes.

```
""" This is the start of the comment
This is another line.
This is the last line in the comment. """
```

Here's another example.

```
"""
I've started this comment down here.
Python will not try to interpret these lines since they are comments.
"""
```

You can even create a single line quote using the triple quote syntax.

```
"""This is yet another comment."""
```

Going back to our "What Does The Cat Say" exercise from the previous chapter, you can add in some comments to make your code clearer.

```
# Get the input from the user.
text = input('What would you like the cat to say? ')

# Determine the length of the input.
text_length = len(text)

# Make the border the same size as the input.
print('        {}'.format('_' * text_length))
print('       < {} >'.format(text))
print('        {}'.format('-' * text_length))
print('       /')
print(' /\_/\ /')
print('( o.o )')
print(' > ^ <')
```

Review

- Unlike strings, numbers require no special decoration.

- If you enclose a number in quotes it is actually a string.

- To convert a string to an integer, use the int( ) function.

- To convert a string to a float, use the float( ) function.

- Single line comments begin with an octothorpe (#).

- Multi-line comments are enclosed in triple quotes (""").

Exercises

Calculate the Cost of Cloud Hosting

Let's assume you are planning to use your Python skills to build a social networking service. You decide to host your application on servers running in the cloud. You pick a hosting provider that charges $0.51 per hour. You will launch your service using one server and want to know how much it will cost to operate per day and per month.

Write a Python program that displays the answers to the following questions:

- How much does it cost to operate one server per day?
- How much does it cost to operate one server per month?

Solution

Here is one way to answer those questions using Python. Notice that comments are used throughout the code. Also, keep in mind there are multiple ways to solve the same problem.

```python
# The cost of one server per hour.
cost_per_hour = 0.51

# Compute the costs for one server.
cost_per_day = 24 * cost_per_hour
cost_per_month = 30 * cost_per_day

# Display the results.
print('Cost to operate one server per day is ${:.2f}.'.format(cost_per_day))
print('Cost to operate one server per month is ${:.2f}.'.format(cost_per_month))
```

Output:

```
Cost to operate one server per day is $12.24.
Cost to operate one server per month is $367.20.
```

Calculate the Cost of Cloud Hosting, Continued

Building on the previous example, let's also assume that you have saved $918 to fund your new adventure. You wonder how many days you can keep one server running before your money runs out. Of course, you hope your social network becomes popular and requires 20 servers to keep up with the demand. How much will it cost to operate at that point?

Write a Python program that displays the answers to the following questions:

- How much does it cost to operate one server per day?

- How much does it cost to operate one server per month?

- How much does it cost to operate twenty servers per day?

- How much does it cost to operate twenty servers per month?

- How many days can I operate one server with $918?

Solution

```python
# The cost of one server per hour.
cost_per_hour = 0.51

# Compute the costs for one server.
cost_per_day = 24 * cost_per_hour
cost_per_month = 30 * cost_per_day

# Compute the costs for twenty servers
cost_per_day_twenty = 20 * cost_per_day
cost_per_month_twenty = 20 * cost_per_month

# Budgeting
budget = 918
operational_days = budget / cost_per_day

# Display the results.
print('Cost to operate one server per day is ${:.2f}.'.format(cost_per_day))
print('Cost to operate one server per month is ${:.2f}.'.format(cost_per_month))
print('Cost to operate twenty servers per day is ${:.2f}.'.format(cost_per_day_twenty))
print('Cost to operate twenty servers per month is ${:.2f}.'.format(cost_per_month_twenty))
print('A server can operate on a ${0:.2f} budget for {1:.0f} days.'.format(budget, operational_days))
```

Output:

```
Cost to operate one server per day is $12.24.
```

Cost to operate one server per month is $367.20.
Cost to operate twenty servers per day is $244.80.
Cost to operate twenty servers per month is $7344.00.
A server can operate on a $918.00 budget for 75 days.

Chapter 3 - Booleans and Conditionals

A boolean is a data type that can have only two possible values: True or False . You can think of a boolean as either being on or off. There is no in between with booleans. To assign a boolean to a variable use variable_name = boolean , where boolean is either True or False . Do not use quotes around True or False . Remember, quotes are for strings.

```
a_boolean = True
the_other_boolean = False
print(a_boolean)
print(the_other_boolean)
```

Output:

```
True
False
```

Comparators

The following six operators compare one numeric value with another and result in a boolean.

Operator	Description
==	Equal to
>	Greater than
>=	Greater than or equal
<	Less than
<=	Less than or equal
!=	Not equal

When you see 1 == 2 you can think "Is 1 equal to 2?". If the answer is yes, then it's True. If the answer is no, then it's False. In this example the answer is no, so the condition is False. Note that = assigns a value to a variable and == performs a comparison.

```
is_one_equal_to_two = 1 == 2
print(is_one_equal_to_two)
```

Output:

```
False
```

Let's run the numbers 1 and 2 through all six comparators interactively in the Python interpreter.

```
>>> 1 == 2
False
>>> 1 > 2
False
>>> 1 >= 2
False
>>> 1 < 2
True
```

```
>>> 1 <= 2
True
>>> 1 != 2
True
```

Boolean Operators

Boolean logic is used extensively in computer programming. The boolean operators are `and`, `or`, and `not`. They can be used to compare two statements or negate a statement. Like comparators, they result in a boolean.

Operator	Description
and	Evaluates to True if both statements are true, otherwise evaluates to False .
or	Evaluates to True if either of the statements is true, otherwise evaluates to False .
not	Evaluates to the opposite of the statement.

The following is a truth table that demonstrates boolean operators and their results.

```
True and True is True
True and False is False
False and True is False
False and False is False

True or True is True
True or False is True
False or True is True
False or False is False

Not True is False
Not False is True
```

Let's evaluate two statements with the boolean and operator. The first statement is 37 > 29 and it evaluates to True . The second statement is 37 < 40 and also evaluates to True . 37 > 29 and 37 < 40 evaluates to True because True and True evaluate to True .

```
>>> 37 > 29
True
>>> 37 < 40
True
>>> 37 > 29 and 37 < 40
True
>>>
```

What is the result of 37 > 29 or 37 < 40 ?

```
>>> 37 > 29 or 37 < 40
True
```

The not boolean operator evaluates to the opposite of the statement. Since 37 > 29 is True , not 37 > 29 is False .

```
>>> 37 > 29
True
>>> not 37 > 29
False
```

The order of operations for boolean operators is:

- not

- and

- or   is   . First   is evaluated and
For example, True and False or not False   True   not False
is True . Next True and False is evaluated and is False . Finally, True or False is
evaluated and is True .

```
>>> not False
True
>>> True and False
False
>>> True or False
True
>>> True and False or not False
True
```

To control the order of operations use parenthesis. Anything surrounded by parenthesis is evaluated first and as its own unit. True and False or not False is the same as (True and False) or (not False) . It's also the same as ((True and False) or (not False)) . Using parenthesis not only allows you to get away with not memorizing the order of operations, but more importantly it is explicit and clear.

Conditionals

The `if` statement evaluates a boolean expression and if it is `True` the code associated with it is executed. Let's look at an example.

```
if 37 < 40:
    print('Thirty-seven is less than forty.')
```

Output:

```
Thirty-seven is less than forty.
```

Since the boolean expression `37 < 40` is `True` the code indented under the `if` statement is executed. This indented code is called a code block. All the statements that are the same distance to the right belong to that code block. A code block can contain one or more lines. The block of code ends when it is followed by a line that is less indented than the current code block. Also, code blocks can be nested. Here is a logical view of code blocks.

```
Block One
    Block Two
    Block Two
        Block Three
Block One
Block One
```

By convention, code blocks are indented using four spaces but this in not strictly enforced. Python allows you to use other levels of indentation. For example, using two spaces for indentation is next most popular choice after four spaces. Be consistent. If you decide to use two spaces for indentation, then use two spaces throughout the program. However, I strongly recommend following the conventions unless you have a good reason not to do so. Also, if you encounter this error you have a problem with spacing.

```
IndentationError: expected an indented block
```

Let's get back to the `if` statement. Notice that the line containing the `if` statement always ends in a colon. Here is another example.

```
age = 31
if age >= 35:
    print('You are old enough to be the President.')

print('Have a nice day!')
```

Output:

```
Have a nice day!
```

Since age >= 35 is False the Python code indented underneath the if statement is not executed. The final print function will always execute because it is outside of the if statement. Notice that it is not indented.

The if statement can be paired with else . The code indented under else will execute when the if statement is false. You can think of the if/else statement meaning, "If the statement is true run the code underneath if , otherwise run the code underneath else ."

```
age = 31
if age >= 35:
    print('You are old enough to be the President.')
else:
    print('You are not old enough to be the President.')

print('Have a nice day!')
```

Output:

```
You are not old enough to be the President.
Have a nice day!
```

You can evaluate multiple conditions by using elif , which is short for "else if." Like if and else , you need to end the line of the elif statement with a colon and indent the code to execute underneath it.

```
age = 31
if age >= 35:
    print('You are old enough to be a Senator or the President.')
elif age >= 30:
    print('You are old enough to be a Senator.')
else:
    print('You are not old enough to be a Senator or the President.')
```

```
print('Have a nice day!')
```

Output:

```
You are old enough to be a Senator.
Have a nice day!
```

Since age >= 3 5 is False , the code underneath the if statement did not execute. Since age >= 3 0 is True the code underneath elif did execute. The code under else will only execute if all of the preceding if and elif statements evaluate to False . Also, the first if or elif statement to evaluate to True will execute and any remaining elif or else blocks will not execute. Here is one final example to illustrate these points.

```
age = 99
if age >= 35:
    print('You are old enough to be a Representative, Senator, or the President.')
elif age >= 30:
    print('You are old enough to be a Senator.')
elif age >= 25:
    print('You are old enough to be a Representative.')
else:
    print('You are not old enough to be a Representative, Senator, or the President.')

print('Have a nice day!')
```

Output:

```
You are old enough to be a Representative, Senator, or the President.
Have a nice day!
```

Review

- Booleans are either True or False.

- Comparators compare one numeric value with another and result in a boolean.

- Boolean operators (and , or , not) compare two statements or negate a statement and result in a boolean.

- Use parenthesis to control the order of operations.

- A code block is a section of code at the same level of indentation.

- Conditionals include if , if/else , and if/elif/else .

Exercises

Walk, Drive, or Fly

Create a program that asks the user how far they want to travel. If they want to travel less than three miles tell them to walk. If they want to travel more than three miles, but less than three hundred miles, tell them to drive. If they want to travel three hundred miles or more tell them to fly.

Sample Output:

```
How far would you like to travel in miles? 2500
I suggest flying to your destination.
```

Solution

```
# Ask for the distance.
distance = input('How far would you like to travel in miles? ')

# Convert the distance to an integer.
distance = int(distance)

# Determine what mode of transport to use.
if distance < 3:
    mode_of_transport = 'walking'
elif distance < 300:
    mode_of_transport = 'driving'
else:
    mode_of_transport = 'flying'

# Display the result.
print('I suggest {} to your destination.'.format(mode_of_transport))
```

Resources

- Built-in Types: https://docs.python.org/3/library/stdtypes.html

- Order of Operations (PEMDAS): http://www.purplemath.com/modules/orderops.htm

- Style Guide for Python Code (PEP 8): http://legacy.python.org/dev/peps/pep-0008/

Chapter 4 - Functions

There is a concept in computer programming known as DRY -- Don't Repeat Yourself. Functions allow you to write a block of Python code once and use it many times. Instead of repeating several lines of code each time you need to perform a particular task, or function, simply call the function that contains that code. This helps in reducing the length of your programs and it also gives you a single place to change, test, troubleshoot, and document a given task. This makes your application easier to maintain.

To create a function use the def keyword followed by the name of the function. A set of parenthesis must follow the function name. If your function accepts parameters include names of those parameters within the parenthesis separated by commas. Finally, end the function definition line with a colon. The code block that follows the function definition will be executed any time the function is called. The format is def function_name(): . Here is a very simple function.

```
def say_hi():
    print('Hi!')
```

If you were to execute this code no output would be displayed because the function was defined but never called. When calling a function be sure to include the parenthesis.

```
def say_hi():
    print('Hi!')
```

```
say_hi()
```

Output:

```
Hi!
```

A function has to be defined before it can be called. Define your functions at the top of your Python program. Here is what happens if you try to use a function that is not yet defined.

```
say_hi()

def say_hi():
    print('Hi!')
```

Output:

```
Traceback (most recent call last):
  File "say_hi.py", line 1, in <module>
    say_hi()
NameError: name 'say_hi' is not defined
```

Let's extend the function to accept a parameter. You can think of parameters as variables that can be used inside of the function. The format is `def function_name(parameter_name): .`

```
def say_hi(name):
    print('Hi {}!'.format(name))

say_hi('Jason')
say_hi('everybody')
```

Output:

```
Hi Jason!
Hi everybody!
```

Once you've defined a parameter the function expects and requires a value for that parameter. If one is not provided you will encounter an error.

```
def say_hi(name):
    print('Hi {}!'.format(name))
```

```
say_hi()
```

Output:

```
File "say_hi.py", line 4, in <module>
  say_hi()
TypeError: say_hi() missing 1 required positional argument: 'name'
```

To make the parameter optional, set a default value for it using the equals sign. The format is def function_name(parameter_name = default_value): .

```
def say_hi(name = 'there'):
  print('Hi {}!'.format(name))

say_hi()
say_hi('Jason')
```

Output:

```
Hi there!
Hi Jason!
```

Functions can accept multiple parameters. Simply include them within the parenthesis of the function definition and separate them with a comma. When calling the function supply the arguments and separate them with a comma as well.

```
def say_hi(first, last):
  print('Hi {} {}!'.format(first, last))

say_hi('Jane', 'Doe')
```

Output:

```
Hi Jane Doe!
```

The parameters accepted by a function are also called positional parameters because their order is important. Notice that Jane was associated with first and Doe was associated with last. You can also explicitly pass values into a function by name. When calling the function supply the parameter name followed by the equals sign and then the value for that parameter. When using named parameters, order is not important. Here's an example.

```
def say_hi(first, last):
    print('Hi {} {}!'.format(first, last))

say_hi(first = 'Jane', last = 'Doe')
say_hi(last = 'Doe', first = 'John')
```

Output:

```
Hi Jane Doe!
Hi John Doe!
```

Required and optional parameters can be combined as in this example.

```
def say_hi(first, last='Doe'):
    print('Hi {} {}!'.format(first, last))

say_hi('Jane')
say_hi('John', 'Coltrane')
```

Output:

```
Hi Jane Doe!
Hi John Coltrane!
```

By convention the first statement of a function is a documentation string, or docstring for short. To create a docstring simply surround text with triple double quotes. This docstring provides a quick summary of the function. When writing the docstring ask yourself, "What does this function do," or "Why does this function exist?" You can access this docstring by using the built-in help() function. Pass the name of the function you want to learn more about to help() . Type q to exit the help screen.

```
def say_hi(first, last='Doe'):
    """Say hello."""
    print('Hi {} {}!'.format(first, last))

help(say_hi)
```

Output:

```
Help on function say_hi in module __main__:

say_hi(first, last='Doe')
    Say hello.
```

Not only can functions perform a task, they can return data using
the return statement. You can return any data type that you like. Once
the return statement is called, no further code in the function is executed.
Here is a function that returns a string.

```
def odd_or_even(number):
    """Determine if a number is odd or even."""
    if number % 2 == 0:
        return 'Even'
    else:
        return 'Odd'

odd_or_even_string = odd_or_even(7)
print(odd_or_even_string)
```

Output:

```
Odd
```

Here is a similar function that returns a boolean.

```
def is_odd(number):
    """Determine if a number is odd."""
    if number % 2 == 0:
        return False
    else:
        return True

print(is_odd(7))
```

Output:

```
True
```

You can create functions that call other functions. Here's an example.

```
def get_name():
    """Get and return a name"""
    name = input('What is your name? ')
```

```
    return name

def say_name(name):
    """Say a name"""
    print('Your name is {}.'.format(name))

def get_and_say_name():
    """Get and display name"""
    name = get_name()
    say_name(name)

get_and_say_name()
```

Output:

```
What is your name? Jason
Your name is Jason.
```

Review

- A function is a block of reusable code that performs an action and can optionally return data.

- A function must be defined before it is called.

- The basic syntax for defining a function is: `def function_name(parameter_name):`.

- A function can accept parameters. To make a parameter optional supply a default value for that parameter.

- You can supply a docstring as the first line of your function.

- The `return` statement exits the function and passes back what follows `return`.

- Use the built-in `help()` function to get help with an object. When supplying a function to `help()` the docstring contained within the function is displayed.

Exercises

Fill in the Blank Word Game

Create a fill in the blank word game. Prompt the user to enter a noun, verb, and an adjective. Use those responses to fill in the blanks and display the story.

- Write a short story. Remove a noun, verb, and an adjective.

- Create a function to get the input from the user.

- Create a function that fills in the blanks in the story you created.

- Ensure each function contains a docstring.

- After the noun, verb, and adjective have been collected from the user, display the story using their input.

Solution

```
def get_word(word_type):
    """Get a word from a user and return that word."""
    if word_type.lower() == 'adjective':
        a_or_an = 'an'
    else:
        a_or_an = 'a'
    return input('Enter a word that is {0} {1}: '.format(a_or_an, word_type))

def fill_in_the_blanks(noun, verb, adjective):
    """Fills in the blanks and returns a completed story."""
    story = "In this book you will learn how to {1}. It's so easy even a {0} can do it. Trust me, it
will be very {2}.".format(noun, verb, adjective)
    return story

def display_story(story):
    """Displays a story."""
    print()
    print('Here is the story you created. Enjoy!')
    print()
    print(story)

def create_story():
    """Creates a story by capturing the input and displaying a finished story."""
    noun = get_word('noun')
    verb = get_word('verb')
    adjective = get_word('adjective')
```

```
        the_story = fill_in_the_blanks(noun, verb, adjective)
        display_story(the_story)

create_story()
```

Output:

```
Enter a word that is a noun: pencil
Enter a word that is a verb: program
Enter a word that is an adjective: important

Here is the story you created. Enjoy!

In this book you will learn how to program. It's so easy even a pencil can do it. Trust me, it will
be very important.
```

Resources

- DRY: https://en.wikipedia.org/wiki/Don%27t_repeat_yourself

- Documentation for the help( ) built-in function: https://docs.python.org/3/library/functions.html#help

- Docstring Conventions (PEP 257): http://legacy.python.org/dev/peps/pep-0257/

Chapter 5 - Lists

So far you have learned about the string, integer, float, and boolean data types. A list is a data type that holds an ordered collection of items. The items, or values, contained in a list can be various data types themselves. You can even have lists within lists.

Lists are created using comma separated values between square brackets. The format is `list_name = [item_1, item_2, item_N]`. To create an empty list use: `list_name = []`. Items in a list can be accessed by index. List indices are zero based, meaning that the first item in the list has an index of 0, the second item has an index of 1, etc. To access an item in a list using an index, enclose the index in square brackets immediately following the list name. The format is `list_name[index]`.

```
animals = ['man', 'bear', 'pig']
print(animals[0])
print(animals[1])
print(animals[2])
```

Output:

```
man
bear
pig
```

Not only can you access values by index, you can also set values by index.

```
animals = ['man', 'bear', 'pig']
```

```
print(animals[0])
animals[0] = 'cat'
print(animals[0])
```

Output:

```
man
cat
```

You can access items starting at the end of the list by using a negative index. The -1 index represents the last item in the list, -2 represents the second to last item in the list, and so on.

```
animals = ['man', 'bear', 'pig']
print(animals[-1])
print(animals[-2])
print(animals[-3])
```

Output:

```
pig
bear
man
```

Adding Items to a List

To add an item to the end of a list use the append() method and pass in the item to add to the list.

```
animals = ['man', 'bear', 'pig']
animals.append('cow')
print(animals[-1])
```

Output:

```
cow
```

To add multiple items to the end of a list, use the extend() method. The extend() method takes a list. You pass in a list by name or create one by surrounding a list of items within brackets.

```
animals = ['man', 'bear', 'pig']
animals.extend(['cow', 'duck'])
print(animals)

more_animals = ['horse', 'dog']
animals.extend(more_animals)
print(animals)
```

Output:

```
['man', 'bear', 'pig', 'cow', 'duck']
['man', 'bear', 'pig', 'cow', 'duck', 'horse', 'dog']
```

You can also add a single item at any point in the list by using the insert() method. Pass in the index where you want to add the item followed by a comma and then the item itself. All of the existing items in the list will be shifted by one.

```
animals = ['man', 'bear', 'pig']
animals.insert(0, 'horse')
print(animals)

animals.insert(2, 'duck')
print(animals)
```

Output:

['horse', 'man', 'bear', 'pig']
['horse', 'man', 'duck', 'bear', 'pig']

Slices

To access a portion of a list, called a slice, specify two indices separated by a colon within brackets. The slice starts at the first index and goes up to, but does not include, the last index. If the first index is omitted 0 is assumed. If the second index is omitted the number of items in the list is assumed.

```
animals = ['man', 'bear', 'pig', 'cow', 'duck', 'horse']

some_animals = animals[1:4]
print('Some animals:     {}'.format(some_animals))

first_two = animals[0:2]
print('First two animals: {}'.format(first_two))

first_two_again = animals[:2]
print('First two animals: {}'.format(first_two_again))

last_two = animals[4:6]
print('Last two animals:  {}'.format(last_two))

last_two_again = animals[-2:]
print('Last two animals:  {}'.format(last_two_again))
```

Output:

```
Some animals:     ['bear', 'pig', 'cow']
First two  animals: ['man', 'bear']
First two animals: ['man', 'bear']
Last two animals: ['duck', 'horse']
Last two animals: ['duck', 'horse']
```

String Slices

You can use slices with strings. You can think of a string as a list of characters.

```
part_of_a_horse = 'horse'[1:3]
print(part_of_a_horse)
```

Output:

```
or
```

Finding an Item in a List

The index() method accepts a value as a parameter and returns the index of the first value in the list. For example, if there were two occurrences of bear in the animals list animals.index('bear') would return the index of the first occurrence of bear. If the value is not found in the list, Python will raise an exception.

```
animals = ['man', 'bear', 'pig']
bear_index = animals.index('bear')
print(bear_index)
```

Output:

```
1
```

Exceptions

An exception is typically an indication that something went wrong or something unexpected occurred in your program. If you don't account for, or handle, exceptions in your program Python will print out a message explaining the exception and halt the execution of the program. Here is an example an unhandled exception.

```
animals = ['man', 'bear', 'pig']
cat_index = animals.index('cat')
print(cat_index)
```

Output:

```
Traceback (most recent call last):
  File "exception_example.py", line 2, in <module>
    cat_index = animals.index('cat')
ValueError: 'cat' is not in list
```

These messages can be extremely useful in correcting mistakes in your code. As you can see from the previous example, Python displayed the line number and code that raised the exception.

To prevent Python from exiting when it encounters an exception you need to tell your program what to do when it encounters one. Surround any code you think may raise an exceptionin a try/except block. Let's update the previous example with a try/except block.

```
animals = ['man', 'bear', 'pig']
try:
    cat_index = animals.index('cat')
except:
    cat_index = 'No cats found.'
print(cat_index)
```

Output:

```
No cats found.
```

If an exception is raised while executing the code in the `try:` code block, the code in the `except:` code block is executed. If no exception is encountered in the `try:` code block, the code in the `except:` code block is skipped and not executed.

Looping through a List

If you want to perform some action on every item in a list, use a for loop. The format is `for item_variable in list_name:` . Like if statements and function definitions, the for statement ends in a colon. The code block that follows the for statement will be executed for every item in the list. Essentially what happens is that the first item in the list, `list[0]` is assigned to `item_variable` and the code block is executed. The next item in the list, `list[1]` is assigned to `item_variable` and the code block is executed. This process continues until the list is exhausted. If there are no items in the list the code block will not be executed.

Here is an example that prints the upper case version of every item in the `animals` list.

```
animals = ['man', 'bear', 'pig']
for animal in animals:
    print(animal.upper())
```

Output:

```
MAN
BEAR
PIG
```

In addition to the for loop Python has a while loop. The format is `while condition:` followed by a code block. As long as the condition evaluates to true the code block following the while statement will execute. Typically the code block will alter a variable that is part of the condition. At some point the condition will evaluate to false and the program continues after the while loop. If the condition never evaluates to false it is an infinite loop. To halt the execute of a Python program type Ctr-c . So, if you accidentally create an infinite loop you can break out of your program with Ctrl-c .

The following example creates an index variable to store an integer and will be used as the index of the animals list. The while loop executes while the index is less than the length of the animals list. During the code block the index variable is incremented by one. The plus-equals operator adds a value to the variable's existing value and assigns the new value to that variable. Using  index += 1 will increment the index variable by one.

```
animals = ['man', 'bear', 'pig', 'cow', 'duck', 'horse', 'dog']

index = 0

while index < len(animals):
    print(animals[index])
    index += 1
```

Output:

```
man
bear
pig
cow
duck
horse
dog
```

Sorting a List

To sort a list call the sort() method on the list without any arguments. It will reorder the current list. If you want to create a new list, use the built-in sorted() function and supply a list as an argument.

```
animals = ['man', 'bear', 'pig']
sorted_animals = sorted(animals)
print('Animals list:          {}'.format(animals))
print('Sorted animals list:    {}'.format(sorted_animals))
animals.sort()
print('Animals after sort method: {}'.format(animals))
```

Output:

```
Animals list:          ['man', 'bear', 'pig']
Sorted animals list:     ['bear', 'man', 'pig']
Animals after sort method: ['bear', 'man', 'pig']
```

List Concatenation

To concatenate, or combine, two or more lists use the plus sign.

```
animals = ['man', 'bear', 'pig']
more_animals = ['cow', 'duck', 'horse']
all_animals = animals + more_animals
print(all_animals)
```

Output:

```
['man', 'bear', 'pig', 'cow', 'duck', 'horse']
```

To determine the number of items in a list use the len() built-in function and pass in a list.

```
animals = ['man', 'bear', 'pig']
print(len(animals))
animals.append('cow')
print(len(animals))
```

Output:

```
3
4
```

Ranges

The built-in range() function generates a list of numbers and is often paired with the for statement. This comes in handy when you want to perform an action a given number of times or when you want to have access to the index of a list.

The range() function requires at least one parameter that represents a stop. By default, range() generates a list that starts at zero and continues up to, but not including, the stop. To generate a list that contains N items, pass N to range() like so: range(N) . For example, to get a list of 3 items use range(3) . The list starts at zero and will contain the numbers 0 , 1 , and 2 .

```
for number in range(3):
    print(number)
```

Output:

```
0
1
2
```

You can specify the start as well as the stop. The format is range(start, stop) . To start a list at one and stop at three, use range(1, 3) . This will generate a list that contains only two items, 1 and 2 .

```
for number in range(1, 3):
    print(number)
1
2
```

In addition to the start and stop parameters the range() function can also accept a step parameter When using all three parameters the list will start at the start value, stop just before the stop value, and increment the list by the step value. If no step value is specified, as in the previous examples, its default value is 1 . Let's generate a list that includes all of the odd numbers from 1 to 10.

```
for number in range(1, 10, 2):
```

```
    print(number)
```

Output:

```
1
3
5
7
9
```

Here is an example of using the range() function with a list to print every other item in a list.

```
animals = ['man', 'bear', 'pig', 'cow', 'duck', 'horse', 'dog']
for number in range(0, len(animals), 2):
    print(animals[number])
```

Output:

```
man
pig
duck
dog
```

Review

- Lists are created using comma separated values between square brackets. The format is list_name = [item_1, item_2, item_N] .

- Items in a list can be accessed by index. List indices are zero based. The format is list_name[index] .

- Access items from the end of the list by using negative indices. The last item in a list is list_name[-1] .

- Add items to a list by using the append( ) or extend( ) list methods.

- Access a portion of a list using a slice. The format is list_name(start, stop)

- The list index( ) method accepts a value as a parameter and returns the index of the first value in the list or an exception if the value is not in the list. The format is list_name.index(value) .

- Loop through a list using a for loop. The format is for item_variable in list_name : followed by a code block.

- The code block in a while loop executes as long as the condition evaluates to true. The format is while condition : followed by a code block.

- To sort a list, use the sort( ) list method or the built-in sorted( ) function.

- The built-in range( ) function generates a list of numbers. The format is range(start, stop, step) .

- Unhandled exceptions cause Python programs to terminate. Handle exceptions using try/except blocks.

Exercises

To-Do List

Create a Python program that captures and displays a person's to-do list. Continually prompt the user for another item until they enter a blank item. After all the items are entered, display the to-do list back to the user.

Sample Output:

```
Enter a task for your to-do list. Press <enter> when done: Buy cat food.
Task added.
Enter a task for your to-do list. Press <enter> when done: Mow the lawn.
Task added.
Enter a task for your to-do list. Press <enter> when done: Take over the world.
Task added.
Enter a task for your to-do list. Press <enter> when done:

Your To-Do List:
- - - - - - - - - - -
Buy cat food.
Mow the lawn.
Take over the world.
```

Solution

```python
# Create a list to hold the to-do tasks.
to_do_list = []
finished = False
while not finished:
    task = input('Enter a task for your to-do list. Press <enter> when done: ')
    if len(task) == 0:
        finished = True
    else:
        to_do_list.append(task)
        print('Task added.')

# Display the to-do list.
print()
print('Your To-Do List:')
print('-' * 16)
for task in to_do_list:
    print(task)
```

Resources

- Data Structures (Lists): https://docs.python.org/3/tutorial/datastructures.html

- Exceptions: https://docs.python.org/3/library/exceptions.html

- For Loops: https://wiki.python.org/moin/ForLoop

- Handling Exceptions: https://wiki.python.org/moin/HandlingExceptions

- Sorted: https://docs.python.org/3/library/functions.html#sorted

- While Loops: https://wiki.python.org/moin/WhileLoop

Chapter 6 - Dictionaries

A dictionary is a data type that holds key-value pairs. These key-value pairs are called items. You will sometimes hear dictionaries referred to as associative arrays, hashes, or hash tables.

Dictionaries are created using comma separated items between curly braces. The item starts with a key, is then followed by a colon, and is concluded with a value. The format is dictionary_name = {key_1: value_1, key_N: value_N} . To create an empty dictionary use: dictionary_name = {} .

Items in a dictionary can be accessed by key. To do so, enclose the key in a bracket immediately following the dictionary name. The format is dictionary_name[key] .

```
contacts = {'Jason': '555-0123', 'Carl': '555-0987'}
jasons_phone = contacts['Jason']
carls_phone = contacts['Carl']

print('Dial {} to call Jason.'.format(jasons_phone))
print('Dial {} to call Carl.'.format(carls_phone))
```

Output:

```
Dial 555-0123 to call Jason.
Dial 555-0987 to call Carl.
```

Not only can you access values by key, you can also set values by key. The format is dictionary_name[key] = value .

```
contacts = {'Jason': '555-0123', 'Carl': '555-0987'}
contacts['Jason'] = '555-0000'
jasons_phone = contacts['Jason']
print('Dial {} to call Jason.'.format(jasons_phone))
```

Output:

```
Dial 555-0000 to call Jason.
```

Adding Items to a Dictionary

You can add new items to a dictionary through assignment. The format is dictionary_name[new_key] = value . To determine the number of items in a dictionary use the len() built-in function and pass in a dictionary.

```
contacts = {'Jason': '555-0123', 'Carl': '555-0987'}
contacts['Tony'] = '555-0570'
print(contacts)
print(len(contacts))
```

Output:

```
{'Jason': '555-0123', 'Carl': '555-0987', 'Tony': '555-0570'}
3
```

Removing Items from a Dictionary

To remove an item from a dictionary use the del statement. The format is del dictionary_name[key] .

```
contacts = {'Jason': '555-0123', 'Carl': '555-0987'}
del contacts['Jason']
print(contacts)
```

Output:

```
{'Carl': '555-0987'}
```

The values stored in a dictionary do not have to be of the same data type. In the following example, the value for the Jason key is a list while the value for the Carl key is a string.

```
contacts = {
    'Jason': ['555-0123', '555-0000'],
    'Carl': '555-0987'
}
print('Jason:')
print(contacts['Jason'])
print('Carl:')
print(contacts['Carl'])
```

Output:

```
Jason:
['555-0123', '555-0000']
Carl:
555-0987
```

When assigning the items to the contacts dictionary additional spaces were used to improve readability. As long as the syntax is followed Python will ignore the extra spaces.

Since the dictionary_name['key_name']stores its associated value, you can act upon it like you would the actual values themselves. For example, let's use a for loop for all of Jason's phone numbers.

```
contacts = {
    'Jason': ['555-0123', '555-0000'],
    'Carl': '555-0987'
}

for number in contacts['Jason']:
    print('Phone: {}'.format(number))
```

Output:

```
Phone: 555-0123
Phone: 555-0000
```

Finding a Key in a Dictionary

If you want to know if a certain key exists in a dictionary you can use the value in dictionary_name.keys() syntax. If the value is a key in the dictionary True is returned. If it is not, then False is returned.

```python
contacts = {
    'Jason': ['555-0123', '555-0000'],
    'Carl': '555-0987'
}

if 'Jason' in contacts.keys():
    print("Jason's phone number is:")
    print(contacts['Jason'][0])

if 'Tony' in contacts.keys():
    print("Tony's phone number is:")
    print(contacts['Tony'][0])
```

Output:

```
Jason's phone number is:
555-0123
```

Notice that 'Jason' in contacts evaluates to True so the code block following the if statement is executed. Since 'Tony' in contacts is false, the code block following that statement does not execute. Since contacts['Jason'] holds a list you can act on it as a list. So, contacts['Jason'][0] returns the first value in the list.

Finding a Value in a Dictionary

The values() dictionary method returns a list of values in the dictionary. Use the value in list syntax to determine if the value exists in the list. If the value is in the list, True is returned. Otherwise False is returned.

```
contacts = {
    'Jason': ['555-0123', '555-0000'],
    'Carl': '555-0987'
}

print ('555-0987' in contacts.values())
```

Output:

```
True
```

Looping through a Dictionary

One format for looping through items in a dictionary is for key_variable in dictionary_name: . The code block that follows the for statement will be executed for every item in the dictionary. To access the value of the item in the for loop, use the dictionary_name[key_variable] format. Unlike lists, dictionaries are unordered. The for loop guarantees that all of the items in the dictionary will be processed, however there is no guarantee in which order they will be processed.

It is very common to name dictionaries using a plural noun, such as contacts. The typical format of the for loop uses the singular form of the dictionary name as the key variable. For example, for contact in contacts: or for person in people: .

```
contacts = {
    'Jason': '555-0123',
    'Carl': '555-0987'
}
for contact in contacts:
    print('The number for {0} is {1}.'.format(contact, contacts[contact]))
```

Output:

```
The number for Carl is 555-0987.
The number for Jason is 555-0123.
```

You can also use two variables when defining a for loop to process items in a dictionary. The first variable will contain the key while the second one will contain the value. The format is for key_variable, value_variable in dictionary_name.items(): .

```
contacts = {'Jason': '555-0123', 'Carl': '555-0987'}
for person, phone_number in contacts.items():
    print('The number for {0} is {1}.'.format(person, phone_number))
```

Output:

```
The number for Carl is 555-0987.
The number for Jason is 555-0123.
```

Nesting Dictionaries

Since values in a dictionary can be anything, you can nest dictionaries. In the following example, names are the keys for the contact dictionary, while `phone` and `email` are the keys used in the nested dictionary. Each person in this contact list has a phone number and an email address. If you want to know Jason's email address you can retrieve that information using `contacts['Jason']['email']`.

Pay close attention to the location of colons, quotation marks, commas, and braces. Using additional white space when coding these types of data structures can help you better understand the data.

```python
contacts = {
   'Jason': {
      'phone': '555-0123',
      'email': 'jason@example.com'
   },
   'Carl': {
      'phone': '555-0987',
      'email': 'carl@example.com'
   }
}

for contact in contacts:
   print("{}'s contact info:".format(contact))
   print(contacts[contact]['phone'])
   print(contacts[contact]['email'])
```

Output:

```
Jason's contact info:
555-0123
jason@example.com
Carl's contact info:
555-0987
carl@example.com
```

Review

- Dictionaries hold key-value pairs, called items. dictionary_name = {key_1: value_1, key_N: value_N}

- Access the values stored in a dictionary by key. dictionary_name[key]

- You can add or change values in a dictionary through assignment. dictionary_name[key] = value

- Remove items from a dictionary using the del statement. del dictionary_name[key]

- To determine if a key exists in a dictionary use the value in dictionary_name syntax, which returns a boolean.

- The values( ) dictionary method returns a list of the values stored in that dictionary.

- Loop through a dictionary using the for key_variable in dictionary_name : syntax.

- Dictionary values can be of any data type, including other dictionaries.

Exercises

Interesting Facts

Create a dictionary that contains a list of people and one interesting fact about each of them. Display each person and their interesting fact to the screen. Next, change a fact about one of the people. Also add an additional person and corresponding fact. Display the new list of people and facts. Run the program multiple times and notice if the order changes.

Sample output:

```
Jeff: Is afraid of clowns.
David: Plays the piano.
Jason: Can fly an airplane.

Jeff: Is afraid of heights.
David: Plays the piano.
Jason: Can fly an airplane.
Jill: Can hula dance.
```

Solution

```python
def display_facts(facts):
    """Displays facts"""
    for fact in facts:
        print('{}: {}'.format(fact, facts[fact]))
    print()

facts = {
    'Jason': 'Can fly an airplane.',
    'Jeff': 'Is afraid of clowns.',
    'David': 'Plays the piano.'
}

display_facts(facts)

facts['Jeff'] = 'Is afraid of heights.'
facts['Jill'] = 'Can hula dance.'

display_facts(facts)
```

Resources

- Data Structures (Dictionaries): https://docs.python.org/3/tutorial/datastructures.html

Chapter 7 - Tuples

A tuple is an immutable list, meaning once it is defined it cannot be changed. With normal lists you can add, remove, and change the values in the list, but with tuples you cannot. Tuples, like lists, are ordered and the values in the tuple can be accessed by index. You can perform many of the same operations on a tuple that you can on a list. You can iterate over the values in a tuple with a for loop, you can concatenate tuples, you can access values from the end of the tuple using negative indices, and you can access slices of a tuple. Tuples are created using comma separated values between parenthesis. The format is tuple_name = (item_1, item_2, item_N) . If you only want a single item in a tuple that single item must be followed by a comma. The format is tuple_name = (item_1,) .

Tuples are great for holding data that will not or should not change during the execution of your program. Using a tuple ensures that the values are not accidentally altered. For example, the days of the week should not change.

```
days_of_the_week = ('Monday', 'Tuesday', 'Wednesday', 'Thursday', 'Friday', 'Saturday', 'Sunday')
monday = days_of_the_week[0]
print(monday)
print()

for day in days_of_the_week:
    print(day)

# You cannot modify values in a tuple. This will raise an exception.
days_of_the_week[0] = 'New Monday'
Monday
```

```
Monday
Tuesday
Wednesday
Thursday
Friday
Saturday
Sunday
Traceback (most recent call last):
  File "tuples.py", line 10, in <module>
    days_of_the_week[0] = 'New Monday'
TypeError: 'tuple' object does not support item assignment
```

Even though you cannot change the values in a tuple, you can remove the entire tuple during the execution of your program by using the   del statement.

```
days_of_the_week = ('Monday', 'Tuesday', 'Wednesday', 'Thursday', 'Friday', 'Saturday', 'Sunday')
print(days_of_the_week)
del days_of_the_week
# This will raise an exception since the tuple was deleted.
print(days_of_the_week)
```

Output:

```
('Monday', 'Tuesday', 'Wednesday', 'Thursday', 'Friday', 'Saturday', 'Sunday')
Traceback (most recent call last):
  File "tuples2.py", line 5, in <module>
    print(days_of_the_week)
NameError: name 'days_of_the_week' is not defined
```

Switching between Tuples and Lists

To create a list from a tuple, use the list() built-in function and pass in the tuple. To create a tuple from a list, use the tuple() built-in function. The built-in function type() will reveal an object's type.

```python
days_of_the_week_tuple = ('Monday', 'Tuesday', 'Wednesday', 'Thursday', 'Friday', 'Saturday', 'Sunday')
days_of_the_week_list = list(days_of_the_week_tuple)
print('days_of_the_week_tuple is {}.'.format(type(days_of_the_week_tuple)))
print('days_of_the_week_list is {}.'.format(type(days_of_the_week_list)))

animals_list = ['man', 'bear', 'pig']
animals_tuple = tuple(animals_list)
print('animals_list is {}.'.format(type(animals_list)))
print('animals_tuple is {}.'.format(type(animals_tuple)))
```

Output:

```
days_of_the_week_tuple is <class 'tuple'>.
days_of_the_week_list is <class 'list'>.
animals_list is <class 'list'>.
animals_tuple is <class 'tuple'>.
```

Looping through a Tuple

If you want to perform some action on every item in a tuple, use a for loop. The format is for item_variable in tuple_name: followed by a code block.

```
days_of_the_week = ('Monday', 'Tuesday', 'Wednesday', 'Thursday', 'Friday', 'Saturday', 'Sunday')
for day in days_of_the_week:
    print(day)
```

Output:

```
Monday
Tuesday
Wednesday
Thursday
Friday
Saturday
Sunday
```

Tuple Assignment

You can use tuples to assign values to multiple variables at once. In the following example, the variables `mon`, `tue`, `wed`, `thr`, `fri`, `sat`, and `sun` are assigned the days of the week from the `days_of_the_week` tuple.

```
days_of_the_week = ('Monday', 'Tuesday', 'Wednesday', 'Thursday', 'Friday', 'Saturday', 'Sunday')
(mon, tue, wed, thr, fri, sat, sun) = days_of_the_week
print(mon)
print(fri)
```

Output:

```
Monday
Friday
```

You can also use tuple assignment with lists.

```
contact_info = ['555-0123', 'jason@example.com']
(phone, email) = contact_info
print(phone)
print(email)
```

Output:

```
555-0123
jason@example.com
```

Tuple assignment can be used with functions as well. For example, you could create a function that returns a tuple and assigns those values to different variables.

The following example uses the built-in `max()` and `min()` functions. The `max()` built-in function returns the largest item that is passed to it.built-The `min()` in function returns the smallest item that is passed to it.

```
def high_and_low(numbers):
    """Determine the highest and lowest number"""
    highest = max(numbers)
    lowest = min(numbers)
    return (highest, lowest)
```

```
lottery_numbers = [16, 4, 42, 15, 23, 8]
(highest, lowest) = high_and_low(lottery_numbers)
print('The highest number is: {}'.format(highest))
print('The lowest number is: {}'.format(lowest))
```

Output:

```
The highest number is: 42
The lowest number is: 4
```

You can use tuple assignment in a for loop. In the following example the contacts list contains a series of tuples. Each time the for loop is executed the variables name and phone are populated with the contents of a tuple from the contacts list.

```
contacts = [('Jason', '555-0123'), ('Carl', '555-0987')]
for (name, phone) in contacts:
    print("{}'s phone number is {}.".format(name, phone))
```

Output:

```
Jason's phone number is 555-0123.
Carl's phone number is 555-0987.
```

Review

- A tuples is an immutable list, meaning once it is defined the values contained in the tuple cannot be changed.

- Delete a tuple with the del statement. del tuple_name

- Tuples can be converted to lists using the list() built-in function.

- Lists can be converted to tuples using the tuple() built-in function.

- You can use tuple assignment to assign values to multiple variables at once. (var_1, var_N) = (value_1, value_N)

- Tuple assignment can be used in for loops.

- The max() built-in function returns the largest item that is passed to it.

- The min() built-in function returns the smallest item that is passed to it.

Exercises

Airport Codes

Create a list of airports that includes a series of tuples containing an airport's name and its code. Loop through the list and utilize tuple assignment. Use one variable to hold the airport name and another variable to hold the airport code. Display the airport's name and code to the screen.

Sample output:

```
The code for O'Hare International Airport is ORD.
The code for Los Angeles International Airport is LAX.
The code for Dallas/Fort Worth International Airport is DFW.
The code for Denver International Airport is DEN.
```

Solution

```python
airports = [
    ("O'Hare International Airport", 'ORD'),
    ('Los Angeles International Airport', 'LAX'),
    ('Dallas/Fort Worth International Airport', 'DFW'),
    ('Denver International Airport', 'DEN')
]

for (airport, code) in airports:
    print('The code for {} is {}.'.format(airport, code))
```

Resources

- list( ) documentation: https://docs.python.org/3/library/functions.html#func-list

- max( ) documentation: https://docs.python.org/3/library/functions.html#max

- min( ) documentation: https://docs.python.org/3/library/functions.html#min

- type( ) documentation: https://docs.python.org/3/library/functions.html#type

- tuple( ) documentation: https://docs.python.org/3/library/functions.html#func-tuple

Chapter 8 - Reading from and Writing to Files

You learned how to accept standard input by using the built-in input() function. You also know how to send data to standard output -- the screen -- using the print() function. Using standard input and output work well for certain types of applications, but if you want to keep data generated by your program you will need a place to store that data. Also, if you want to retrieve saved data, you will need techniques to do that as well. One common place to store data is a file. You can read input and write output to a file, just like you can read input from a keyboard and display output on a screen.

To open a file, use the built-in open() function. The format is open(path_to_file) . The path_to_file can be an absolute or a relative path and it includes the file name. An absolute path contains the entire path starting at the root of the file system, be that a / in Mac or Linux or a drive letter in Windows. An example of an absolute path is /var/log/messages . A relative path will contain just the file name or a portion of the path which starts at the current working directory. An example relative path is log/messages . This example assumes the current working directory is /var .

Using forward slashes as a directory separator will be familiar to those that have ever worked on a Unix or Unix-like operating system. However, Python recognizes forward slashes even when running on the Windows operating system. The Windows operating system uses back slashes as the directory separator. For example, C:/Users/jason/Documents/python-notes.txt is a valid absolute path in Python. Also, Documents/python-notes.txt is a valid relative path.

The open() function returns a file object, sometimes referred to as a stream object, which can be used to perform operations on the file passed to the open() function. To read the entire file in at once, use the read() method on the file object. The read() method returns a string containing the file's contents. Here is an example.

```
hosts = open('/etc/hosts')
hosts_file_contents = hosts.read()
print(hosts_file_contents)
```

Output:

```
127.0.0.1 localhost
```

To modify the previous example to work on a Windows system, set the hosts variable to C:/Windows/System32/drivers/etc/hosts' .

```
hosts = open('C:/Windows/System32/drivers/etc/hosts')
```

File Position

When reading from a file, Python keeps track of your current position in the file. Since the read() method returns the entire file, the current position will be at the end of the file. If you call read() again, an empty string will be returned since there is no more data to return at your current position in the file. To change the current file position, use the seek() method and pass in a byte offset. For example, to go back to the beginning of the file, use seek(0) . To start at the fifth byte of the file, use seek(5) . Note that in most cases the Nth byte will correspond to the Nth character in the file. However, in some cases it will not. For UTF-8 encoded files you can encounter characters that are longer than one byte. You will run into this situation when using Kanji, Korean, or Chinese. To determine your current position in the file, use the tell() method.

```
hosts = open('/etc/hosts')
print('Current position: {}'.format(hosts.tell()))
print(hosts.read())

print('Current position: {}'.format(hosts.tell()))
print(hosts.read())

hosts.seek(0)
print('Current position: {}'.format(hosts.tell()))
print(hosts.read())
```

Output:

```
Current position: 0
127.0.0.1 localhost

Current position: 20

Current position: 0
127.0.0.1 localhost
```

The read() method can accept the number of characters to read. The following example will display the first three characters of the hosts file. In this case, the first three characters are also first three bytes.

```
hosts = open('/etc/hosts')
```

```
print(hosts.read(3))
print(hosts.tell())
```

Output:

```
127
3
```

Closing a File

It is a good practice to close a file once you are done with it. If your Python application opens many files during its execution this could lead to a "Too many open files" error. To close a file, use the close() method on the file object.

```
hosts = open('/etc/hosts')
hosts_file_contents = hosts.read()
print(hosts_file_contents)
hosts.close()
```

Output:

```
127.0.0.1 localhost
```

Each file object has a closed attribute that returns True if the file is closed and False if it is not. You can use this attribute to ensure a file is closed.

```
hosts = open('/etc/hosts')
hosts_file_contents = hosts.read()
print('File closed? {}'.format(hosts.closed))
if not hosts.closed:
    hosts.close()
print('File closed? {}'.format(hosts.closed))
```

Output:

```
File closed? False
File closed? True
```

Automatically Closing a File

To automatically close a file use the with statement. The format is with open(file_path) as file_object_variable_name: followed by a code block. When the code block finishes Python will automatically close the file. Also, if the code block is interrupted for any reason, including an exception, the file is closed.

```python
print('Started reading the file.')
with open('/etc/hosts') as hosts:
    print('File closed?  {}'.format(hosts.closed))
    print(hosts.read())
print('Finished reading the file.')
print('File closed?  {}'.format(hosts.closed))
```

Output:

```
Started reading the file.
File closed? False
127.0.0.1 localhost
Finished reading the file.
File closed? True
```

Reading a File One Line at a Time

To read a file one line at a time, use a `for` loop. The format is `for line_variable in file_object_variable`: followed by a code block.

```
with open('file.txt') as the_file:
    for line in the_file:
        print(line)
```

Output:

```
This is line one.

This is line two.

Finally, we are on the third and last line of the file.
```

The contents of file.txt :

```
This is line one.
This is line two.
Finally, we are on the third and last line of the file.
```

In the output there is a blank line between each one of the lines in the file. This is because the `line` variable contains the complete line from the file which includes a carriage return, or new line, character. To remove any trailing white space, including the new line and carriage return characters, use the `rstrip()` string method.

```
with open('file.txt') as the_file:
    for line in the_file:
        print(line.rstrip())
```

Output:

```
This is line one.
This is line two.
Finally, we are on the third and last line of the file.
```

File Modes

When opening a file you can specify a mode. The format is open(path_to_file, mode) . So far we have been using the default file mode of r which opens a file in read-only mode. If you want to write to a file, clearing any of its existing contents, use the w mode. If you want to create a new file and write to it, use the x mode. If the file already exists an exception will be raised. Using the x mode prevents you from accidentally overwriting existing files. If you want keep the contents of an existing file and append, or add, additional data to it, use the a mode. With both the w and a modes, if the file does not already exist it will be created. If you want to read and write to the same file, use the + mode.

Mode	Description
r	Open for reading (default)
w	Open for writing, truncating the file first
x	Create a new file and open it for writing
a	Open for writing, appending to the end of the file if it exists
b	Binary mode
t	Text mode (default)
+	Open a disk file for updating (reading and writing)

You can also specify if the file you are working with is a text file or a binary file. By default, all files are opened as text files unless otherwise specified. Simply append a t or b to one of the read or write modes. For instance, to open a file for reading in binary mode use rb . To append to a binary file use ab .

Text files contain strings while binary files contain a series of bytes. Said another way, text files are human readable and binary files are not. Examples of binary files include images, videos, and compressed files.

To check the current mode of a file, use the `mode` attribute on a file object.

```
with open('file.txt') as the_file:
    print(the_file.mode)
```

Output:

```
r
```

Writing to a File

Now that you know about the different file modes, let's write some data to a file. It's as easy as calling the write() method on the file object and supplying the text you wish to write to the file.

```
with open('file2.txt', 'w') as the_file:
    the_file.write('This text will be written to the file.')
    the_file.write('Here is more text.')

with open('file2.txt') as the_file:
    print(the_file.read())
```

Output:

```
This text will be written to the file.Here is more text.
```

The output might not be what you expected. The write() method writes exactly what was provided to the file. In the previous example no carriage return or line feed was provided so all the text ended up on the same line. The \r sequence represents the carriage return character and \n represents a new line. Let's try the example again, but this time using a line feed character at the end of the line.

```
with open('file2.txt', 'w') as the_file:
    the_file.write('This text will be written to the file.\n')
    the_file.write('Here is more text.\n')

with open('file2.txt') as the_file:
    print(the_file.read())
```

Output:

```
This text will be written to the file.
Here is more text.
```

Unix style line endings only contain the \n character. Mac and Linux files use this type of line ending. Windows style line endings can be created by using \r\n .

Binary Files

The main thing to remember about binary files is that you are dealing with bytes, not characters. The read() method accepts bytes as an argument when dealing with binary files. Remember that the read() method accepts characters when the file is opened as a text file.

```
with open('cat.jpg', 'rb') as cat_picture:
    cat_picture.seek(2)
    cat_picture.read(4)
    print(cat_picture.tell())
    print(cat_picture.mode)
```

Output:

```
6
rb
```

Exceptions

Working with anything that exists outside of your program increases the chances for errors and exceptions. Working with files falls well within this category. For example, a file you are attempting to write to may be read-only. A file you are attempting to read from may not be available. In a previous chapter you learned about the try/except block. Let's put it to use in the following example.

```python
# Open a file and assign its contents to a variable.
# If the file is unavailable, create an empty variable.
try:
    contacts = open('contacts.txt').read()
except:
    contacts = []


print(len(contacts))
```

Output:

```
3
```

If the file could not be read, the output would be:

```
0
```

Review

- To open a file, use the built-in open() function. The format is open(path_to_file, mode) .

- If mode is omitted when opening a file it defaults to read-only.

- Forward slashes can be used as directory separators, even in Windows.

- The read( ) file object method returns the entire contents of the file as a string.

- To close a file, use the close( ) file object method.

- To automatically close a file use the with statement. The format is with open(file_path) as file_object_variable_name : followed by a code block.

- To read a file one line at a time, use a for loop. The format is for line_variable in file_object_variable : .

- To remove any trailing white space use the rstrip( ) string method.

- Write data to a file using the write( ) file object method.

- When a file is opened in binary mode, the read( ) file object accepts bytes. When a file is opened in text mode, which is the default, read( ) accepts characters.

- In most cases a character is one byte in the length, but this does not hold true in every situation.

- Plan for exceptions when working with files. Use try/except blocks.

Exercises

Line Numbers

Create a program that opens file.txt . Read each line of the file and prepend it with a line number.

Sample output:

```
1: This is line one.
2: This is line two.
3: Finally, we are on the third and last line of the file.
```

Solution

```
with open('file.txt') as file:
    line_number = 1
    for line in file:
        print('{}: {}'.format(line_number, line.rstrip()))
        line_number += 1
```

Alphabetize

Read the contents of animals.txt and produce a file named animals-sorted.txt that is sorted alphabetically.

The contents of animals.txt :

```
man
bear
pig
cow
duck
horse
dog
```

After the program is executed the contents of animals-sorted.txt should be:

```
bear
cow
dog
duck
horse
```

```
man
pig
```

Solution

```python
unsorted_file_name = 'animals.txt'
sorted_file_name = 'animals-sorted.txt'
animals = []

try:
    with open(unsorted_file_name) as animals_file:
        for line in animals_file:
            animals.append(line)
    animals.sort()
except:
    print('Could not open {}.'.format(unsorted_file_name))

try:
    with open(sorted_file_name, 'w') as animals_sorted_file:
        for animal in animals:
            animals_sorted_file.write(animal)
except:
    print('Could not open {}.'.format(sorted_file_name))
```

Resources

- Core tools for working with streams: https://docs.python.org/3/library/io.html

- Handling Exceptions: https://wiki.python.org/moin/HandlingExceptions

- open() documentation: https://docs.python.org/3/library/functions.html#open

Chapter 9 - Modules and the Python Standard Library

Modules

Python modules are files that have a .py extension and can implement a set of attributes (variables), methods (functions), and classes (types). A module can be included in another Python program by using the import statement followed by the module name. To import a module named time include import time in your Python program. You can now access the methods within the time module by calling time.method_name( ) or attributes, sometimes called variables, by calling time.attribute_name . Here is an example using the asctime( ) method and the timezone attribute from the time module. The timezone attribute contains the number of seconds between UTC and the local time.

```
import time
print(time.asctime())
print(time.timezone)
```

Output:

```
Mon Aug 25 19:08:43 2014
21600
```

When you import module_name , all of the methods in that module are available as module_name.method_name( ) . If you want to use a single method in a module you can import just that method using the from module_name import method_name syntax. Now the method is available in your program by name. Instead of calling module_name.method_name() you can now call method_name() .

```
from time import asctime
print(asctime())
```

Output:

```
Mon Aug 25 19:08:43 2014
```

You can do the same thing with module attributes and classes. If you want to import more than one item from a module you can create a separate from module_name import method_name line for each one. You can also provide a comma separated list like this: from module_name import method_name1, method_name2, method_name N . Let's import the asctime() and sleep() methods from time time module. The sleep() method suspends execution for a given number of seconds.

```
from time import asctime, sleep
print(asctime())
sleep(3)
print(asctime())
```

Output:

```
Mon Aug 25 19:08:43 2014
Mon Aug 25 19:08:46 2014
```

One of the advantages of importing a single method or list of methods from a module is that you can access it directly by name without having to precede it with the module name. For example, sleep(3) versus time.sleep(3) . If you want to be able to access everything from a module use an asterisk instead of a list of methods to import. However, I do not recommend this practice. I only point it out because you will see it used from time to time. The reason you want to avoid this approach is that if you import everything into your program you may override an existing function or variable. Also, if you import multiple methods using an asterisk it will make it hard to determine what came from where.

```
from time import *
print(timezone)
print(asctime())
sleep(3)
print(asctime())
```

Output:

```
21600
Mon Aug 25 19:08:43 2014
Mon Aug 25 19:08:46 2014
```

Peeking Inside a Module

Use the dir() built-in function to find out what attributes, methods, and classes exist within a module.

```
>>> import time
>>> dir(time)
['_STRUCT_TM_ITEMS', '__doc__', '__file__', '__loader__', '__name__', '__package__',
'__spec__', 'altzone', 'asctime', 'clock', 'ctime', 'daylight', 'get_clock_info', 'gmtime', 'localtime',
'mktime', 'monotonic', 'perf_counter', 'process_time', 'sleep', 'strftime', 'strptime', 'struct_time',
'time', 'timezone', 'tzname', 'tzset']
```

The Module Search Path

You can view the default module search path by examining sys.path . When you issue an import module_name statement, Python looks for the module in the first path in the list. If it is not found the next path is examined and so on until the module is found or all of the module search paths are exhausted. In addition to directories, the module search path may include zip files. Python will search within the zip file file for a matching module as well. The default module search path will vary depending on your installation of Python, the Python version, and the operating system. Here is an example from a Python installation on a Mac.

```
# show_module_path.py
import sys
for path in sys.path:
    print(path)
```

Output:

```
/Users/jason
/Library/Frameworks/Python.framework/Versions/3.4/lib/python34.zip
/Library/Frameworks/Python.framework/Versions/3.4/lib/python3.4
/Library/Frameworks/Python.framework/Versions/3.4/lib/python3.4/plat-darwin
/Library/Frameworks/Python.framework/Versions/3.4/lib/python3.4/lib-dynload
/Library/Frameworks/Python.framework/Versions/3.4/lib/python3.4/site-packages
```

The show_module_path.py file was located in /Users/j when I executed python3 show_module_path.py . Notice that /Users/j is first in the module search path. The other directories were determined by the Python installation.

If you want Python to look in other locations for modules you will need to manipulate the module search path. There are two methods to do this. The first method is to modify sys.path as you would any other list. For example, you can append directory locations using a string data type.

```
import sys
sys.path.append('/Users/jason/python')
for path in sys.path:
    print(path)
```

Output:

```
/Users/jason
/Library/Frameworks/Python.framework/Versions/3.4/lib/python34.zip
/Library/Frameworks/Python.framework/Versions/3.4/lib/python3.4
/Library/Frameworks/Python.framework/Versions/3.4/lib/python3.4/plat-darwin
/Library/Frameworks/Python.framework/Versions/3.4/lib/python3.4/lib-dynload
/Library/Frameworks/Python.framework/Versions/3.4/lib/python3.4/site-packages
/Users/jason/python
```

You can also manipulate the PYTHONPATH environment variable. It acts very similar to the PATH environment variable. On Mac and Linux systems PYTHONPATH can be populated with a list of colon separated directories. On Windows systems the PYTHONPATH environment variable requires the use of a semicolon to separate the list of directories. The directories listed in PYTHONPATH are inserted after the directory where the script resides and before the default module search path.

In this example /Users/jason is the directory where the show_module_path.py Python program resides. The /Users/jason/python and /usr/local/python/modules paths are included in PYTHONPATH. The export command makes PYTHONPATH available to programs started from the shell.

```
[jason@mac ~]$ export PYTHONPATH=/Users/jason/python:/usr/local/python/modules
[jason@mac ~]$ pwd
/Users/jason
[jason@mac ~]$ python3 show_module_path.py
/Users/jason
/Users/jason/python
/usr/local/python/modules
/Library/Frameworks/Python.framework/Versions/3.4/lib/python34.zip
/Library/Frameworks/Python.framework/Versions/3.4/lib/python3.4
/Library/Frameworks/Python.framework/Versions/3.4/lib/python3.4/plat-darwin
/Library/Frameworks/Python.framework/Versions/3.4/lib/python3.4/lib-dynload
/Library/Frameworks/Python.framework/Versions/3.4/lib/python3.4/site-packages
[jason@mac ~]$
```

If a module is not found in the search path an ImportError exception is raised.

```
import say_hi
```

Output:

```
Traceback (most recent call last):
  File "test_say_hi.py", line 1, in <module>
    import say_hi
ImportError: No module named 'say_hi'
```

The Python Standard Library

In the previous examples we have been using the time module which is included with Python. Python is distributed with a large library of modules that you can take advantage of. As a matter of fact, I suggest looking at what the Python standard library has to offer before writing any of your own code. For example, if you want to read and write CSV (comma-separated values) files don't waste your time reinventing the wheel. Simply use Python's csv module. Do you want to enable logging in your program? Use the logging module. Do you want to make an HTTP request to a web service and then parse the JSON response? Use the urllib.request and json modules. The list of what is available in the Python Standard Library is located at https://docs.python.org/3/library/.

Let's use the exit() method from the sys module to cleanly terminate a program if we encounter an error. In the following example the file test.txt is opened. If the program encounters an error opening the file the code block following except: will execute. If the reading of test.txt is required for the remaining program to function correctly, there is no need to continue. The exit() method can take an exit code as an argument. If no exit code is provided, 0 is used. By convention, when an error causes a program to exit a non-zero exit code is expected.

```python
import sys
file_name = 'test.txt'
try:
    with open(file_name) as test_file:
        for line in test_file:
            print(line)
except:
    print('Could not open {}.'.format(file_name))
    sys.exit(1)
```

Creating Your Own Modules

Just as Python has a library of reusable code, so can you. If you want to create your own module, it's easy. Remember that in the simplest form, modules are files that have a .py extension. Simply create a Python file with your code and import it from another Python program.

Here are the contents of say_hi.py .

```
def say_hi():
    print('Hi!')
```

Here is how you can import and use the say_hi module. To call the say_hi() method within the say_hi module, use say_hi.say_hi() .

```
import say_hi
say_hi.say_hi()
```

Output:

```
Hi!
```

This is another simple module called say_hi2 . Here are the contents of say_hi2.py .

```
def say_hi():
    print('Hi!')

print('Hello from say_hi2.py!')
```

Let's see what happens when you import the say_hi2 module.

```
import say_hi2
say_hi2.say_hi()
```

Output:

```
Hello from say_hi2.py!
Hi!
```

What happened? When say_hi2 is imported its contents are executed. First, the say_hi() function is defined. Next the print function is executed. Python allows you to create programs that behave one way when they are executed and another way when they are imported. If you want to be able to reuse functions from an existing Python program but do not want the main program to execute, you can account for that.

Using main

When a Python file is executed as a program the special variable __name__ is set to __main__ . When it is imported the __name__ variable is not populated. You can use this to control the behavior of your Python program. Here is the say_hi3.py file.

```python
def say_hi():
    print('Hi!')

def main():
    print('Hello from say_hi3.py!')
    say_hi()

if __name__ == '_main_':
    main()
```

When it is executed as a program the code block following if __name__ == '_main_': is executed. In this example it simply calls main() . This is a common pattern and you will see this in many Python applications. When say_hi3.py is imported as a module nothing is executed unless explicitly called from the importing program.

```
[jason@mac ~]$ python3 say_hi3.py
Hello from say_hi3.py!
Hi!
[jason@mac ~]$
```

Output:

```
Hi!
```

Review

- Python modules are files that have a .py extension and can implement a set of variables, functions, and classes.

- Use the import module_name syntax to import a module.

- The default module search path is determined by your Python installation.

- To manipulate the module search path modify sys.path or set the PYTHONPATH environment variable.

- The Python standard library is a large collection of code that can be reused in your Python programs.

- Use the dir() built-in function to find out what exists within a module.

- You can create your own personal library by writing your own modules.

- You can control how a Python program behaves based on whether it is run interactively or imported by checking the value of ___name_ _ .

- The if __name__ == '__main__': syntax is a common Python idiom.

Exercises

What Did the Cat Say, Redux

Update the "What Did the Cat Say" program from Chapter 1 so that it can be run directly or imported as a module. When it runs as a program is should prompt for input and display a cat "saying" what was provided by the user. Place the input provided by the user inside a speech bubble. Make the speech bubble expand or contract to fit around the input provided by the user.

Sample output when run interactively:

```
         _____
     < Pet me and I will purr. >
         - - - - - - - - - - - - - -
         /
   ∧_∧ /
   ( o.o )
   > ^ <
```

Next, create a new program called cat_talk.py that imports the cat_say module. Use a function from the cat_say() module to display various messages to the screen.

Sample output when used as a module:

```
         _____
     < Feed me. >
         - - - - - .
         /
   ∧_∧ /
   ( o.o )
   > ^ <

         _____
     < Pet me. >
         - - - - -
         /
   ∧_∧ /
   ( o.o )
   > ^ <

         _____
     < Purr. Purr. >
```

```
     --------
    /
  /\_/\ /
 ( o.o )
  > ^ <
```

Solution

Here are the contents of cat_say.py :

```python
def cat_say(text):
    """Generate a picture of a cat saying something"""
    text_length = len(text)
    print('          {}'.format('_' * text_length))
    print('        < {} >'.format(text))
    print('          {}'.format('-' * text_length))
    print('        /')
    print(' /\_/\ /')
    print('( o.o )')
    print(' > ^ <')


def main():
    text = input('What would you like the cat to say? ')
    cat_say(text)


if __name__ == '__main__':
    main()
```

Here are the contents of cat_talk.py :

```python
import cat_say

def main():
    cat_say.cat_say('Feed me.')
    cat_say.cat_say('Pet me.')
    cat_say.cat_say('Purr. Purr.')

if __name__ == '__main__':
    main()
```

Resources

- __main__ documentation: https://docs.python.org/3/library/__main__.html

- Idioms and Anti-Idioms in Python: https://docs.python.org/3/howto/doanddont.html

- Linux for Beginners: http://www.linuxtrainingacademy.com/linux.

- PYTHONPATH documentation: https://docs.python.org/3/using/cmdline.html#envvar-PYTHONPATH

- The Python Standard Library: https://docs.python.org/3/library/

- The sys module: https://docs.python.org/3/library/sys.html

- sys.path documentation: https://docs.python.org/3/library/sys.html#sys.path

- virtualenv documentation: https://pypi.python.org/pypi/virtualenv

Conclusion

Even though this is the end of this book, I sincerely hope that it is just the beginning of your Python journey. Python has been growing steadily in popularity over the last decade and is increasingly used in all areas of computing. You will find Python powering popular websites such as Pinterest, Instagram, and Reddit. Python is used in scientific computing and is running on supercomputers around the world. It's used for system administration tasks like configuration and package management with YUM and anaconda being prime examples. Python has been used to create popular games such as *EVE Online* and *Toontown* . No matter what your programming interests, the possibilities for learning, exploring, and growing are endless.

Here's one last Python program.

```
import this
```

Output:

```
The Zen of Python, by Tim Peters

Beautiful is better than ugly.
Explicit is better than implicit.
Simple is better than complex.
Complex is better than complicated.
Flat is better than nested.
Sparse is better than dense.
Readability counts.
Special cases aren't special enough to break the rules.
Although practicality beats purity.
Errors should never pass silently.
Unless explicitly silenced.
In the face of ambiguity, refuse the temptation to guess.
There should be one-- and preferably only one --obvious way to do it.
Although that way may not be obvious at first unless you're Dutch.
Now is better than never.
Although never is often better than *right* now.
If the implementation is hard to explain, it's a bad idea.
If the implementation is easy to explain, it may be a good idea.
Namespaces are one honking great idea -- let's do more of those!
```

Appendix

Appendix A: Trademarks

BSD/OS is a trademark of Berkeley Software Design, Inc. in the United States and other countries.

Linux® is the registered trademark of Linus Torvalds in the U.S. and other countries.

Mac and OS X are trademarks of Apple Inc., registered in the U.S. and other countries.

Open Source is a registered certification mark of Open Source Initiative.

Python is a registered trademark of the Python Software Foundation.

UNIX is a registered trademark of The Open Group.

Windows is a registered trademark of Microsoft Corporation in the United States and other countries.

All other product names mentioned herein are the trademarks of their respective owners.

CPSIA information can be obtained
at www.ICGtesting.com
Printed in the USA
BVHW050904160621
609639BV00005B/1280